MOUNTAIN BIKING
The Complete Guide

Sports Illustrated Winner's Circle Books

BOOKS ON TEAM SPORTS

Baseball
Basketball
Football: Winning Defense
Football: Winning Offense
Hockey
Lacrosse
Pitching
Soccer

BOOKS ON INDIVIDUAL SPORTS

Bowling
Competitive Swimming
Cross-Country Skiing
Figure Skating
Golf
Racquetball
Running for Women
Skiing
Tennis
Track: Championship Running
Track: The Field Events

SPECIAL BOOKS

Backpacking
Canoeing
Fly Fishing
Mountain Biking
Scuba Diving
Small-Boat Sailing
Strength Training
Training with Weights

Sports Illustrated

MOUNTAIN BIKING

The Complete Guide

by Bob Woodward

Photography by Bill Jaspersohn and Bob Woodward

Sports Illustrated

Winner's Circle Books
New York

Special thanks to Bellweather, Inc., Gary Bonacker, Joe Breeze, Bridgestone Cycle (USA), Inc., Susan Conner, Wende Cragg, Gary Fisher, Fisher Mountain Bikes, Don Leet, Nike, Inc., John Platt, Bob Rogen, Sunnyside Sports, Jim Terhaar, Paul Thomasberg–Team Giant, Trek USA, Walter, and Chip.

Every effort has been made in this book's preparation to stress the need for proper technique and safety when riding a mountain bike. Before beginning any bicycling program, however, check with your health care practitioner to make sure it is appropriate for you to start such a program. Follow all instructions carefully, and be aware that using the equipment discussed in this book could result in physical injury or even death, for which the author, photographers, Sports Illustrated Winner's Circle Books, and Time, Inc., will not be responsible.

Photo Credits: Bob Ward, pp. 12, 178; Wende Cregg, pp. 21, 209, 210; Gary Fisher Bicycle Company, pp. 24, 115, 206, 208 (top); Chequamegon Fat Tire Festival, Hayward, Wisconsin, pp. 212 (bottom), 213 (top and middle); Phil Van Valkenberg, p. 213 (bottom); Mt. Snow, Vermont, pp. 181, 215; National Archives, Washington, D.C., p. 19; Joe Breeze, p. 23; Specialized Bicycle Components, pp. 25, 37 (top); Bridgestone Cycle (USA), p. 140; West Virginia Department of Commerce, p. 182; Kevin Mireles, p. 199; *Crested Butte Chronicle,* p. 208; Backroads Bicycle Touring–Tom Hale, p. 183; Backroads Bicycle Touring–Dennis Coello, p. 200; Gordon Wiltsie, p. 220 (top). Cover by Bob Woodward. All other photographs by Bill Jaspersohn and Bob Woodward.

FIRST EDITION

Designer: Kim Llewellyn

Library of Congress Cataloging-in-Publication Data

Woodward, Bob.
  Sports illustrated mountain biking: the complete guide / by Bob Woodward; photography by Bill Jaspersohn and Bob Woodward.

    p. cm.—(Sports illustrated winner's circle books)
  ISBN 0-452-26652-1
    1. All terrain cycling.   I. Sports illustrated (Time, Inc.)   II. Title.
  III. Series.
  GV1056.W67   1991   796.6–dc20   91-7363

  ISBN 0–452–26652–1   91 92 93 94 95 AG/HL 10 9 8 7 6 5 4 3 2 1

To my klunker bike mentor, Ted Eugenis; to Phil Meglasson and George Macaluso for discovering the joys of mountain biking with me; and to Dennis Heater for keeping the spirit alive.

Contents

MOUNTAIN BIKING
The Complete Guide

Introduction

Fourteen years ago I read a magazine story about a group of bicycle enthusiasts in Marin County, California, who were taking old fat-tire bikes, which they had nicknamed "klunkers," and were using them for off-road trail riding. The idea was instantly appealing to me because my most memorable, and often disastrous, rides on the trusty fat-tire Schwinn of my childhood had been off-road.

About the time my interest was piqued, my friend and longtime bicycle riding companion Ted Eugenis also got wind of the fat-tire revolution. We phoned bike builders in Marin, and before long we had added gears and drum brakes to two old klunkers acquired at a rummage sale.

Then we took our creations out on the trails and logging roads of Bend, Oregon, where we live, and found ourselves beating them and our bodies to a figurative pulp—and loving every minute of the bashing. Afterward we'd talk about the riding techniques that seemed to work for the different trail conditions we'd encountered, and we tinkered endlessly, trying to come up with better gearing, better tires, better brakes.

A few months later, when on assignment in San Francisco, I took some time to go to Marin County to visit three entrepreneurs—Gary Fisher, Tom Ritchey, and Charlie Kelly—who were making what they called a "mountain bike." The company was Kelly-Fisher MountainBikes, and an hour's discussion at a local espresso bar with Charlie, their marketing person, was enough to convince me that their 15-speed, specially designed machine was the bike of the future.

Then Kelly let me try one. After riding a heavy, cumbersome, unrespon-

The bottom line on mountain biking is that it lets you
have fun while taking you almost anywhere.

sive 1952 Buick of a bike for two years, on the mountain bike I felt as if I were riding a Ferrari Testa Rossa. I was hooked.

Today, nine bikes of my own later, I've covered some incredible back-country terrain on a mountain bike, used one for touring on three continents, raced them, commuted on them, and had some of the best times of my life on them. In the process, I've stayed in shape and done a lot of grinning. After all, the bottom line with mountain biking is that it's fun and it lets the kid within you out to play.

The purpose of this book is not only to share my enthusiasm for the sport but also to offer, in a simple, straightforward manner, the basics of mountain biking technique and riding possibilities. I won't dazzle you with technical data but instead will lay a foundation on which you can build your personal riding technique through experience.

HOW TO USE THIS BOOK

The object of this book is to illustrate the basics of mountain biking. That means practical equipment, riding, and maintenance tips along with personal anecdotes to keep the going lively.

Perhaps the most difficult part of writing about mountain biking is trying to keep up to date on the information about equipment. For that reason I offer equipment basics, knowing full well that by the time you read this there may be countless innovations in gearing, handlebars, chainstays, and other components. The creative energy that surrounds mountain bike manufacturing today is impressive. Every year the bicycle trade shows are jammed with new gizmos and gadgets, all purported to make your riding better. Some are flashes in the pan; others really do enhance riding pleasure. With this book you will be able to become familiar with the essentials of the mountain bike; thereafter you should rely on a good bicycle specialty shop to keep you informed about the latest technological changes and innovations.

Every chapter here should be viewed as a starting point for further exploration. For example, the information in the chapter on riding technique will prove invaluable when you're getting started. Once you've done a fair amount of riding, you'll find yourself adapting these basic techniques or adopting others of your own invention.

A note on the photos: to fully illustrate every nuance of technique, maintenance steps, and repair procedures would fill a book twice this size. Again, as with the text, think of the photographs as primers to help focus your creative energies on how best to ride, repair, and maintain your mountain bike.

This is a book for self-starters, doers, people who aren't afraid to be left to their own devices once they have the basics down. Use it as a solid foundation for years of mountain bike riding enjoyment.

1

America's Bicycle

Mountain bikes are as American as apple pie, the Stars and Stripes, hot dogs, and fireworks on the Fourth of July. They are the product of American ingenuity, with their origin reaching back to our nation's earliest bicycles.

For the past sixty years or so, American bicycles have moved along the roads on fat tires. (By contrast, European bikes typically have been thin-tire models built more along racing bike lines.) The sturdy, wide-tire bike has historically been the riders' bike of choice, two notable exceptions to this preference being our Olympic racing hopefuls and the famous six-day indoor competition riders of the 1890s. Sociologists and techno-historians can probably provide a dozen reasons for this; I like to think it has something to do with the American way of building heavy, durable equipment.

A MILITARY FOREBEAR

The modern-day mountain bike is the direct descendent of the military bicycle used by the U.S. Army's Twenty-fifth Bicycle Corps Regiment in the late 1890s. The Corps' weighty (90-pound) off-road bikes were looked upon as promising tactical warfare vehicles for messenger service and lightning-strike skirmishes. The April 1896 issue of *Harper's Magazine* carried a story extolling the use of bicycles by the military: "It is in rapidly moving considerable bodies of infantry that the bicycle will find its highest function in time of war. Fancy a force of infantry, independent of roads and railroads, moving in any direction, forty or fifty miles in one morning, and appearing on a field not weary and exhausted after two days march, but fresh and prepared to fight."

From their base in Ft. Missoula, Montana, the Twenty-fifth made lengthy

Fat tires and wide-open spaces—that's cycling the American way.

forays into Montana and Yellowstone National Park to prove the worth of man and machine. Then on June 14, 1897, the Corps left Ft. Missoula on their bikes for a 1,900-mile trip to St. Louis. This arduous journey through Montana, Wyoming, South Dakota, and Nebraska would show military leaders in Washington, D.C., that bicycles were indeed war-worthy.

Forty-one days later, the bicycle troops arrived to a heroes' welcome in St. Louis. They had endured every hardship imaginable, from severe weather to numerous mechanical breakdowns, hunger, and lack of water. The men carried their complete kit and weapons, and though now weak and tired, they had averaged 46 miles a day.

Unfortunately the bicycle never became the popular military vehicle that people thought it would. Yet bicycles have been used in every major 20th-century conflict, and today some countries—Switzerland, for example—still maintain a bicycle corps.

THE AMERICAN MAINSTREAM

Long after the demise of the Twenty-fifth Bicycle Corps, American manufacturers continued to make sturdy machines. The heavy, stable American bike became the two-wheel equivalent of the big, boaty cars that automobile companies produced in the 1950s and '60s.

Our archetypal American bike is the one ridden by the newsboys and delivery boys of Norman Rockwell's Americana. It's the bike that the boy in Andrew Wyeth's painting *Young America* rides, with a raccoon tail flying from its whip antenna.

Drawing on this legacy of balloon-tire bicycles, a small group of active cyclists created the modern mountain bike in the mid and late 1970s, and in doing so ushered in a new era of cycling for riders of all ages. But before telling that story, let's meet one of bicycling's modern-day pioneers.

John Finley Scott

In every sport there is someone who has an idea whose time hasn't come, a precursor who may be viewed as odd during his time but later is acknowledged as having been something of a visionary. John Finley Scott is such a person.

Scott may not be the father of the modern mountain bike, but long before the term was coined, he was exploring California's backcountry on a multi-geared off-road two-wheel vehicle of his own creation.

Soldiers of the Twenty-fifth Bicycle Corps, ready for duty, June 1897.

In 1953 this native Californian and avid cyclist was a student at Reed College, near Portland, Oregon. "I observed that the bike made the most sense for off-road travel and set about building up one for that purpose," Scott recalls.

He found a diamond frame that would accommodate balloon tires, selected a variety of road bike components (four-speed Sturmey-Archer gearing, Weinman side-pull brakes, standard European flat touring handlebars), and created his off-road bike.

For three years Scott toured the wilds of Oregon and California, until his custom rear wheel was stolen in 1956. Six years later, he saw some French 650B touring tires and was inspired to create another off-road model. Scott says, "During the next nineteen years, I did an incredible amount of exploration by bike." Those trips included the first bicycle ascents of California's White Mountain, Yosemite's Half Dome, and Telescope Peak in Nevada. The bike he used is still in working order at his home in Davis, California.

In the mid-1970s Scott got to know bike builders Gary Fisher and Tom Ritchey, and helped finance their efforts in creating the first production mountain bikes. To him, then, we owe a debt of gratitude for his vision, inventiveness, and timely support of a budding industry when it most needed the help.

Today John Finley Scott is a member of the sociology faculty at the University of California, Davis, still a passionate cyclist, and a living chapter in the history of American cycling.

Mt. Tam to Mass Production

The fat-tire/mountain bike craze began inconspicuously enough, in 1974, near the Marin County, California, towns of Mill Valley and Larkspur. A group of Velo Club–Tamalpais bicycle racers—including Gary Fisher, Joe Breeze, Otis Guy, and Charlie Kelly, along with another area racer, Tom Ritchey—bought all the old balloon-tire, coaster-brake Schwinn newsboy bikes they could find, fixed them up, and used them to cruise around town. Soon they tired of cruising and went looking for new kicks.

Since both Larkspur and Mill Valley are nestled on the flanks of Mt. Tamalpais, it seemed logical to truck the fat-tire bikes up to the top of the 2,600-foot peak and ride downhill. A local fad began. Mt. Tamalpais is laced with a network of trails and fire roads, and it soon became the mecca for downhill fat-tire bike riding. But there were a few uphills along the routes down, and these perplexed riders until Gary Fisher, a bike shop mechanic, changed the game. "I got fed up with pushing my bike uphill," he recalls, "so I started putting BMX parts—gears and things like drum brakes—on my old

Mountain biking in its infancy: Otis Guy off-road on Marin County's Mt. Tamalpais.

Schwinns." Fisher's first ecletic bikes were greeted with scorn. "The other riders thought it was blasphemous," Fisher remembers, laughing, "but a few weeks later they were on Mt. Tam with their Schwinns all done up with new gadgets."

Thus the fat-tire downhill game became an all-terrain riding game. The bikes became known as klunkers, and a San Francisco television station won a national award for a documentary on "klunking" in Marin. The world was becoming aware of off-road riding. But what they didn't see or hear about was

"Klunkers" and "ballooners," circa 1979.

the toll on bike frames. Soon every available old Schwinn bike frame in the Bay Area seemed to have been bought and trashed.

In 1977 Fisher's friend Joe Breeze built ten chrome-moly steel frames modeled after the famous Schwinn Excelsior X frame (chrome-moly is a light, durable steel made with traces of chrome and molybdenum). They were snapped up immediately by fat-tire fanatics. Another Marin rider, Don Koski, designed a different frame called the Pro Cruiser, which eventually gained wide acceptance among fellow riders, especially after well-known local motorcyclist

Joe Breeze's 1977 "Breezer," one of the first bikes built with chrome-moly steel to withstand off-road punishment.

Mert Lawill took over their production. For many, the Pro Cruiser was the ultimate downhill machine, with cantilever hand brakes, 5-speed gearing, and a rugged frame. At $350, the Pro Cruiser might have been the first successfully mass-produced mountain bike, had not so many come a cropper due to component failures.

Frame design and component innovation continued at a feverish pace in back yards and back rooms. Don Koski's brother Erik designed and produced the Trailmaster, which became a megahit with fat-tire riders in 1978. Then in 1979 the game changed again, and this time forever, when Tom Ritchey designed the first MountainBike frame. Outfitted by Gary Fisher and his partner Charles Kelly, the all-steel frame could withstand virtually every physical abuse it was subjected to.

A bike design fanatic and former racer, Ritchey deviated from the current design norm, dropping the popular Schwinn cantilever frame configuration and substituting a diamond shape like that used on standard thin-tire road bicycles. From that day forward, the components Fisher added would become de rigueur for mountain bikes: 15-speed gearing, heavy-duty cantilever brakes, quick-release seat post, alloy rim wheels, and fat knobby tires.

The mountain bike's founding father, Gary Fisher, strikes his version of the corporate executive pose in 1980.

Priced between $1,300 and $1,500, the MountainBike didn't exactly turn fat-tire bicycling into America's fastest-growing sport, but it did open more eyes to the pastime. Of course cynics scoffed. Wasn't this just another Marin County fad, like group therapy, hot tubs, and personal gurus?

Watching these developments was Mike Sinyard of Specialized Bicycle Components. Sinyard envisioned the fat-tire bike as the great all-purpose self-propelled vehicle, but he realized it had to come down in price to be accepted. He contracted to have fat-tire bicycles (now known generically as mountain bikes because of the Ritchey machine) made in the Far East, and in 1982 he introduced his Stumpjumper model. Sinyard's Stumpjumper was the first moderately priced ($650) machine to come to market, and it debuted almost simultaneously with the rise in public interest in off-road riding.

From 1982 to the present, the increase in mountain bike sales has been

The 1982 Stumpjumper—the first mass-appeal mountain bike.

meteoric. Dozens of companies now manufacture frames and components, and according to figures from the Interbike group, mountain bikes accounted for 45 percent (4.5 to 5 million units) of all bicycle sales in the U.S. in 1990. Industry experts estimate that there are now 10 to 15 million mountain bikes in the country, and their riders are not all hard-core hotshots, either. *Average* folk are getting on mountain bikes. Take a look.

A WIDESPREAD APPEAL

Too often the mountain bike enthusiast is pictured as a young, hard-riding daredevil. While it's true that the originators of the vehicle and the first wave of zealots were a bit extreme, the growth of the sport beyond a cult following and beyond racing has seen it embraced by people of all abilities, sensibilities, and ages for general recreation and transportation.

People are attracted to the mountain bike for many reasons. Most important, perhaps, we Americans relate easily to fat tires. They connote a stable ride. Their knobby treads look as if they can withstand a lot of punishment (and they do).

Then there's the mountain bike frame. It's sturdier than the road bike frame. The aura surrounding a mountain bike is much like the one surrounding a Jeep or a Land Rover. These are sensibly built vehicles that, like their motorized counterparts, can travel the roughest roads and actually look better with a good splattering of mud.

Then there's the versatility of the machine. It doesn't restrict you to paved roads the way other bikes do. Every unposted trail, logging road, or back road is fair game for exploring. And be warned: once you ride the back roads and the trails, you'll find it hard to come back to traffic-clogged streets, with their attendant noise and pollution. As you'll quickly discover, fat-tire fun is off-road fun.

Now, if you're wavering about whether mountain biking is right for you, keep in mind that mountain bikes are ridden by a complete cross-section of people. Thousands use their mountain bikes to commute to work, to make long road tours, to find a common bond with their friends and families. Seniors cart their mountain bikes on their motor homes and ride them for exercise wherever they stop; the Seattle and Boston police departments use them to patrol downtown beats; and athletes of all stripes have found mountain biking to be a great way to maintain cardiovascular conditioning and muscle tone.

As important as physical conditioning is to all of us, though, to me the nicest aspect of mountain biking is that it lets us get in touch with the child within each of us. Let that child out and you're bound to have a terrific ride every time, whether it's to the grocery store for a quart of milk or down some mountain path on an all-day tour.

The right bike and the right selection of clothing and accessories enhance the riding experience.

2

Fat-Tire Basics

Of the many types of bikes sold in America, the two most popular styles are road bikes and mountain bikes. Road bikes are also called "10-speed" bikes (a misnomer in this era of 18- to 21-speed gearing), "racing bikes," and "touring bikes." Mountain bikes are always called mountain bikes, despite attempts by some to have them categorized as all-terrain bicycles (ATBs).

The differences between the two bikes are easy to see. The stock road bike comes with thin, virtually smooth, tires, drop handlebars (the ones that look like ram's horns), and gear shifters most often attached to the down tube (the one nearest the rider's lower legs). A road bike is designed for moving over concrete and asphalt roads with a minimum of resistance.

The mountain bike, on the other hand, has fat tires with knobby treads, flat handlebars, shifters on the handlebars, and a quick-release seat post. This is a machine for dirt roads, rocky trails, sand, mud, and any other off-road obstacles. With its beefier frame and components, a typical mountain bike will weigh around 28 pounds, which is about 6 pounds heavier than a road bike of comparable frame size.

For years, steel was the chief frame material used in both types of bike. With time and technological innovation, lighter chrome-moly steel became the standard. Today, mountain and road bike frames are made from a variety of materials including chrome-moly steel, aluminum, titanium, and composite (any two materials, such as carbon fiber and epoxy). Even thinner-walled, lighter, yet still tough versions of chrome-moly such as Prestige and Logic are used on expensive top-of-the-line mountain bike frames.

It's at the top end where most frame material innovations take place. Large-diameter aluminum tubing, introduced first by Klein and later by Can-

Road Bikes and Mountain Bikes

The road bike.

The mountain bike.

nondale, and then quickly adopted by many other companies, has become the second most popular material for mountain bike frame construction.

Within the past four years, the experimenters, always in search of a lighter frame that retains strenth and resiliency, have begun using titanium and composites (carbon fiber/Kevlar). As long as bike makers' creative juices keep flowing, count on yearly innovations in frame materials.

Still, with all the innovation, it's hard to fault what have become old standbys: chrome-moly steel and aluminum. There are arguments as to why one works better than the other, but I feel that the merits of each can be determined only after years of personal use. When shopping for a mountain bike, try riding models made of different materials, and trust your sense of "feel" as to which suits you best. If, however, you want something exotic and fancy yourself an experimenter, and you have money to spend, include one of the exotic-frame bikes, made of titanium or carbon fiber, in your test rides. They're light, tough, and—you've been warned—expensive.

A GEOMETRY LESSON

No talk about frames is complete without reviewing the most important aspect of frame design: its geometry. Frame geometry is all a matter of angles and lengths. As one mountain bike manufacturer said when asked about mountain bike technology in the decade of the 1990s, "People can come up with the most unusual components, the most radical new materials, but it's still the geometry of the bike that makes it a good or bad ride."

When we talk geometry, what do we need to know? Only the basics. Geometrically speaking, the mountain bike consists of a main triangle and a rear triangle. The main triangle contains the three most important elements of the frame: the top tube, the seat tube, and the down tube. The front forks are attached to the head tube to complete the front end of the frame. The rear triangle includes the seatstay, the chainstay, the front and rear dropouts, and the bottom bracket. (The dropouts are where the wheels are inserted and held in place, and the bottom bracket holds the pedal crank arms.)

There are two key geometric angles to consider when looking at a mountain bike: the head tube angle and the seat tube angle. Key measurements to consider are top tube and chainstay lengths.

There are a few generalities that can be made about these angles and measurements, but caution is in order: there are also so many tiny variables tied into each key angle and measurement that sweeping declarations are presump-

Anatomy of a Mountain Bike

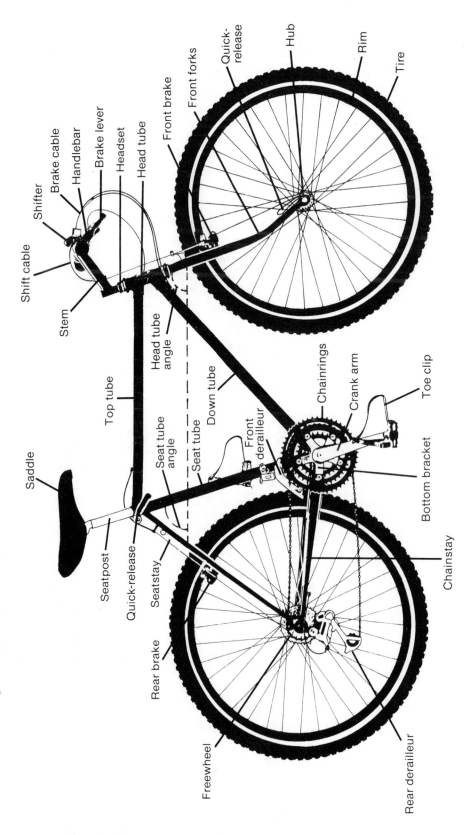

Shift cable
Shifter
Brake cable
Handlebar
Brake lever
Headset
Head tube
Front brake
Front forks
Quick-release
Hub
Rim
Tire

Stem
Head tube angle
Top tube
Seat tube angle
Seat tube
Down tube
Front derailleur
Chainrings
Crank arm
Toe clip
Bottom bracket

Saddle
Seatpost
Quick-release
Seatstay
Rear brake
Freewheel
Chainstay
Rear derailleur

tuous. Here's a safe generalization, though: the steeper the head tube angle (71 to 73 degrees), the quicker-reacting the bike; the shallower the angle (68 to 70 degrees), the slower-reacting the bike. Another generalization about angles: the steeper the seat post angle (72 to 74 degrees), the more direct the power to the pedals; the shallower (less than 72 degrees), the less power to the pedals.

Want some generalizations about top tube and chainstay measurements? Okay. The longer the top tube (21 to 23 inches, increasing in length with the bike's frame size), the better the overall ride, handling, and rider position; the shorter the chainstay (17 inches and under), the better the bike will climb.

Having stated those generalities, I should note that there have been countless changes in frame geometry over the years. The first mountain bikes were designed for downhill cruising, and as a result had what was referred to as a "laid-back" geometry, with low-angled head (68-degree) and seat (68- to 70-degree) tubes. These bikes also had long top tubes and long (18- to 19-inch) chainstays. These characteristics made for slow-reacting, stable bikes.

As riders improved and their riding took on interesting uphill and tricky downhill challenges, they discovered they needed bikes with faster-reacting front ends, bikes whose front wheels didn't lift up off the ground during a steep climb and whose rear wheel didn't slip around when the rear brake was applied on steep descents.

Frame designers responded with more erect (that is, more vertical) head tubes. This translated immediately into bikes with faster, more maneuverable front ends. They then made the seat angles more upright, not only to help the rider transfer more power directly down onto the pedals but also to distribute the rider's weight more evenly over the entire bike so that it wouldn't be rear-end heavy. With the rider's weight more evenly distributed, rear wheel slide was reduced on downhills, and front wheel buck was reduced on steep ascents.

Shortened chainstays, along with the more upright seat tube and rider position, translated into more direct power to the rear wheel for climbing and became a factor in reduced rear wheel washout on braked descents.

Another small but key ingredient in the frame design changes was the reduction of the offset of the front fork. Straightening the fork and head tube angles made for a much faster steering machine.

As the mountain bike industry grew, there was progress and there were problems. In their rush to change, most bike manufacturers shortened their frames' top tubes, rationalizing that a shorter tube would mean a less stretched-out rider. According to their logic, in a more compressed riding position, the rider's body weight would be more centered over the bike and would give him far better bike control. Head tube angles went as high as 73 degrees, seat tubes as high as 74 degrees, while top tubes were trimmed to 20 inches and chainstays were shortened as far as mechanically possible, creating mountain bikes that were overly fast-reacting, unstable, and for all but the smallest riders, physically cramping.

Slowly the bike makers began to recognize their errors, and today they have standardized those angles that make for a stable, fast-reacting bike that climbs and descends well. If you go looking for a new mountain bike, it's good to have an idea of general angle and length specifications: head tube angle, between 70 and 72 degrees; seat tube angle, between 72 and 74 degrees; top tube length (increases with the frame size), between 21 and 23 inches; chainstays, under 17 inches; fork rake, between 1¾ and 2 inches.

Among the other items you might like to remember when you go bike shopping is bottom bracket height. Most bikes have an 11½-inch-high bottom bracket, but there are bikes with ones that measure as high as 13 inches. The higher the bottom bracket, the better the riding clearance over logs, boulders, and other trail obstructions. A higher bottom bracket transfers more weight to the rear wheel while you are climbing, which can be a real help, but also puts more weight on the front wheel in steep descents, which can cause trouble.

The higher bottom bracket also means a slightly tippier, harder-to-handle bike at high speeds. Conversely, a lower bottom bracket equals a stable machine, but one that can get hung up when you try to ride it over obstructions.

COMPONENTRY

A bike frame is nothing more than the blank canvas onto which the elements—in this case, components—are added to make the picture complete. Let's start filling out the mountain bike frame with wheels and tires.

Wheels and Tires

Most early mountain bikes had rugged, heavy, steel wheels, but as time went by and bikes and metal alloys improved, the mountain bikes worth owning had aluminum alloy rims. Alloy rims are lightweight, tough, and worth the extra cost.

If any element of mountain biking has changed more dramatically than others since the first production bikes came to market, it has been the tires. Originally bike makers used whatever knobby-tread tires they could find; some dated back to the newsboy-bike era. But as time went by and the sport developed, the width of the tires, the materials from which they're made, and their tread patterns changed.

I tried every available fat (2.125-inch-wide) tire on my first bike. Some gripped well but didn't corner well, and some did just the opposite. A tire from those days that sticks in my mind was the "Snake Belly," whose tread pattern on a dirt trail looked as if a large python were on the loose. Snake Bellies had yellow sidewalls. Anyone could ride tires with black or white sidewalls, but yellow sidewalls—now that was chic.

As with everything I ever learned about mountain bikes, the rumblings came up from California: in 1983 we heard that Tom Ritchey had created a new tire that had revolutionized riding. It was narrower (1.9 inches), so there was less rolling resistance; it had a center alternating lug pattern that helped climbing; and the extra gripper pattern along the edge of the tire gave solid purchase on corners. As soon as these Ritchey "Quad" tires arrived at a local retailer, I bought a pair, installed them on my wheels, and instantly noticed a big improvement in the way the bike handled. And their relative lightness, due to their narrower profile, was a welcome plus.

A couple of years later, Specialized Bicycle Components of Morgan Hill, California, came out with their famous "Ground Control" tire, with its deep row of gripper tread down the tire's middle and sharp rows of gripper teeth at the edges for corner hold. Shortly thereafter Gary Fisher introduced his Fattrax

Two typical off-road tread configurations.
Some treads work better than others in certain terrains. The easiest way to find out which tread works for you: go to a reputable mountain bike shop and test-ride bikes with different tires.

tires, which have the same tread shape and pattern as the most popular off-road motorcycle tires.

The next step in development came in the form of a lightweight version of the Ground Control, made with a bead (the section of the tire that adheres to the rim) of Kevlar instead of the standard steel. Using lightweight, durable Kevlar (also used in bulletproof vests, steel-belted radial tires, and state-of-the-art kayaks and canoes) made not only for lightweight, tough tires but also ones that were easy to remove to repair flats. The racers opened their wallets, and soon Kevlar tires became a mountain bike racing norm.

Since the introduction of Kevlar, tires have gone through still more adaptations, most of them in tread patterns. Ritchey, Fisher, Specialized, Marin (the makers of a tire called the Rockstar), IRC, Tioga (makers of Farmer John tires), have all added to their number of models. As tires have gotten lighter and more technical in their tread pattern, there has been a concomitant swing back to the fat, fat, fat tires that cushion the ride so nicely and are superior in soft sand and dirt. More fat tires (up to 2½ inches) are coming to market, and for the experienced rider the challenge is to match the right tires to the type of riding he or she does most.

Most experienced riders use different front and rear tires. For mine, I use a Ritchey Mega Bite on the rear; it seems to grip as well as any tire I've used. On the front wheel I use a Fisher Fattrax because I like the way it corners. The more you experiment with tires, the more likely you'll find yourself using a different make and model for each wheel.

Getting Tubed

Inflating those knobby tires requires a tube. There are all varieties of tubes, from inexpensive rubber models to expensive, supposedly pinch-proof latex tubes. ("Pinch" refers to the two rattlesnake-bite-like punctures that can occur when the tire gets pinched between two immovable objects. It's the most common cause of off-road flats.)

For most riders a tube is a tube is a tube. I agree with that view—except when it comes to tube valve stems, where there's a major difference. You can buy tubes with either a Schrader (car-tire type) valve or a Presta valve. The Presta valve is the European bicycle tube valve.

The Schrader valve has a pin inside the valve opening, which when depressed allows inflation or deflation. The Presta valve has a nozzle head that unscrews and has to be depressed to allow air to escape from or enter the tube. The Presta valve is easier to operate, lighter, stronger, and less prone to leaks— and therefore gets my vote.

Valves

The Schrader valve.

The Presta valve, which gets the author's vote as the valve of choice.

Playing the Brakes

When the Marin County boys started fooling around, adding to their cruiser bikes to turn them into mountain bikes, they first used rear drum brakes along with a front cantilever brake. But when the motorcyclists-turned-bicyclists got involved in adding components to their cruiser bikes, they insisted on using heavy-duty cantilever brakes for both wheels.

Cantilever brakes are attached high on the front fork and rear seatstay. The brake assemblies on each side of the tire's rim are connected by a cable to the main cable, which goes to the brake levers on the handlebars. When you squeeze the brake lever, the main cable tightens and the brake assemblies close

Properly adjusted, cantilever brakes are time-tested and reliable.

This small brake lever is designed for control by two or three fingers.

like jaws onto the wheel rim to slow or stop the bike. Cantilever brakes are simple and have been time-tested on bikes of all descriptions. On better mountain bikes they are now standard equipment. This standardization came after manufacturers experimented with other concepts like the "Roller Cam" brake and the "U Brake," both often mounted beneath the chainstays in what was thought to give riders better braking in muddy and wet situations. Neither brake was universally accepted as they were hard to adjust, difficult to open to fix a flat, and proved no better than a cantilever brake in wet, muddy situations.

The contemporary cantilever brake grips firmly, is easy to open to allow a wheel to be removed from the bike, and as we'll see in Chapter 15, is a cinch to adjust and repair. Look for cantilevers when you go shopping for a bike.

Gearing Up

The two main elements in a mountain bike's gearing are the chainrings and the gear clusters. Chainrings are the sprocket rings attached to the pedal crank arms. On a mountain bike there are three rings for the three ranges of pedaling action. The large ring is used when the terrain is flat or downhill and the rider wants to go for speed. The middle chainring is somewhat smaller and is used when riding in mixed, rolling terrain. The small inner chainring is used for climbing; it allows the rider's legs to pedal quickly, under less resistance, during ascents.

The chainrings work in conjunction with the gear cluster mounted on the rear wheel. Most such clusters usually have six to seven gears; the smaller gears (identifiable by the smaller number of teeth) are used in conjunction with the middle and outer chainrings for pedal power. The larger gears (more teeth) are normally used for climbing. When you hear an experienced rider say he was riding 48-12, it means he was using his large front chainring (48 teeth) and his small (12-tooth) rear gear. This rider was into a leg-pounding sprint.

The bike's gearing is linked by a chain and controlled by thumb shifters. Cables from the thumb shifters connect to the front and rear derailleurs, which in turn move the chain. The front derailleur moves the chain over the three chainrings; the rear derailleur moves the chain over the gear cluster.

The first mountain bikes were often 3-speed models, many equipped with ancient Sturmey-Archer shifters and derailleurs like those used on the English schoolboy's bike. It wasn't long before mountain bikers had added full gearing, similar to a road bike's, with shifters that, under pressure, would set the derailleur into action.

That was fine until the late 1980s, when on-demand click shifting came into road bicycling and was soon adapted to mountain biking. On-demand click shifting is now standard on most mountain bikes and works like this: instead of using thumb pressure to move from one gear to another, the rider simply clicks the shifter to a desired position and the shift is completed. A combination of a specially designed and integrated gear cluster, chain, rear derailleur, and derailleur cables is necessary to make on-demand click shifting work properly.

Which brings us to the shifters themselves. On a mountain bike the rider is seated upright over straight handlebars. Obviously it is impractical to have to reach down to the bike's frame to shift gears, à la road cycling gears. Accordingly, mountain bikes have always had thumb-operated shifters located a few millimeters inside the handlebar grips.

Thumb shifters allow you to maintain a grip on your handlebars while

The drive train.
Here is a typical mountain bike drive train, with the front derailleur above the chainrings, the rear derailleur below the rear gear cluster.

shifting. The right-hand shifter connects to the rear derailleur and the left-hand one connects to the front (the chainring derailleur).

Until recently, the basic thumb shifter was installed on top of the handlebars. You pushed forward with your thumb to shift up, and back with your index finger to shift down. Simple, effective, and easy to operate, even with gloved hands. Recently, however, there has been a trend toward push-push shifters (two levers per shifter unit) installed under the handlebars. You push one lever to shift up and the other to shift down. The idea is good and is being refined to make it even better.

Shifters

A typical top shifter. (Note the four-finger brake lever.)

Push-push shifters are usually located under the handlebars.

Bars/Saddles/Pedals

Mountain bike handlebars are straight bars fitting into a stem which in turn fits into the bike's headset. When we talk about fit, we'll discuss more about the bars and the stem. Suffice it to say here that flat bars are better than drop bars for climbing and all-around bike control.

Moving back along the top tube we come to the seatpost and the saddle. The seatpost is usually made of sturdy alloy steel or aluminum, and should be easily adjustable up or down (you usually lower your seat for long difficult downhills to get your center of gravity down) by a quick-release mechanism at the top of the seat tube. Atop the seatpost is the saddle, which is like those used on road bikes. Don't think for one minute that an extra-wide saddle or a specially padded saddle will make riding easier on your rear. The best saddle is a leather or synthetic model that is worn in over a period of time to conform to the special shape of your backside. With riding experience, you'll find that good technique does more to save your rear than padded seats or padded clothing.

Last on the mountain bike component list are the pedals. The modern mountain bike pedal is made of a lightweight alloy and has serrated ridges designed to grip the soles of your cycling shoes. As we get into special components, you'll see how important certain additions to the pedals can be to your riding.

Those Special Extras

Among the standard extras on most mountain bikes are braze-ons that allow you to attach a water bottle cage on your seat tube, down tube, or both.

Most important among add-on extras are toe clips. Toe-clip assemblies consist of a steel or plastic cage that fits over the front of the pedal, encasing the toe area of the riding shoe, and a leather or synthetic strap that cinches down over the top of the instep. The mere mention of toe clips usually brings a look of panic from inexperienced riders, whose expression screams, "I don't want to be tied into my bike! I want to be able to step off if things get out of control!" But listen carefully: One of the main reasons for having toe clips installed on your pedals is for better bike control. Toe clips keep your feet in contact with the pedals, and that's important for better ascents, descents, and cornering. Also, without toe clips most riders tend to complete only half the pedaling rotation. The proper pedal motion is a complete circle, consisting of downward push and upward pull. Without the feet linked snugly to the pedals

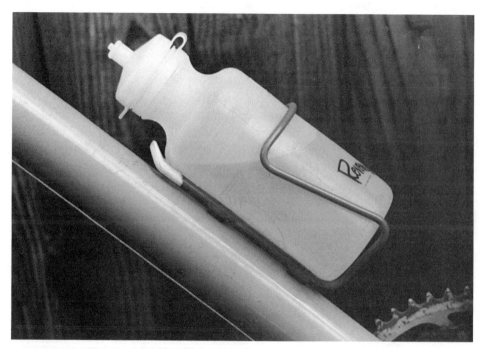

Most mountain bikes come with braze-on clips on either the seat tube or the down tube, to which a water-bottle cage can be attached.

A toe-clip assembly provides better pedaling efficiency and bike control.

with toe clips, the only pedaling power you achieve is during the downward pushing motion. In short, toe clips are essential for deriving the most efficient power from every revolution of the chainrings.

If you're still leery of toe clips but accept their importance in attaining pedal power, try using the clips without the straps until they feel comfortable to you.

Later, as we get into riding footwear, you'll see the importance of having a stiff-soled shoe tied in with toe clips for the utmost pedaling efficiency. We'll also later explore "clipless" pedal systems more throroughly than the cursory look that follows.

For decades a rigid riding shoe with a cleat that snugged down into the pedal was used, along with toe clips, to anchor the top bicycle racer to his bike. However, a few years back, riders in the Tour de France and other major road-race events started using "clipless" shoe systems. Their shoes were fitted with special cleats that fit into specially designed pedals—no toe clips, no toe-clip straps. All it took to get locked into or free of the pedals was a twist of the foot.

Today all but a few road racers go "clipless" because of the on/off ease and the extremely tight link of rider to pedals. A growing number of mountain bike riders are going with "clipless" shoe systems too, but by and large, they have not gained the acceptance of off-road riders because until recently the cleats were raised so far off the shoe's sole that walking or hiking in the shoes was virtually impossible. That's changing with the introduction of specially designed "clipless" mountain bike shoe models, where the cleats are recessed into the soles to allow the rider to walk around.

I would say: don't consider them until you have become an experienced off-road rider. If, however, you do 95 percent of your fat-tire riding on paved roads, going "clipless" makes sense.

Esoterica

Moving on to the more esoteric add-ons, there are mini-chainrings that can be added as a fourth ring to make ascents even easier. These so-called hyper-granny gears let your legs pedal like crazy and seem to help flatten out those sharply angled uphills.

For descents, consider adding a Hite-Rite, a quick-release system that allows you to lower your seat on steep descents and then, with a flick of the wrist, raise the seat back up to its normal height. The Hite-Rite spring connects to the quick-release system and the seat tube. When you open the quick-release, your weight pushes the saddle down as far as you want it to go. Saddle down, you close the quick-release lever and this locks the saddle in place. At the bottom of the descent, just flip open the quick-release, and as you stand up on the pedals with your rear off the saddle, the spring raises the saddle to its preset upper position and you're set for normal flat and mixed-terrain riding.

The Flexstem was invented to reduce shock on the arms, no matter what type of terrain you're covering. It's a complete stem assembly that pivots up and down against an elastoner bushing. Say you're riding along a bumpy road. Normally, when you hit a rock or rut, the shock is driven up though the fork to the handlebars, where it's absorbed by your arms and shoulders. With the Flexstem, the handlebars flex downward as you hit a bump, rock, or depression, and as they do, the shock is absorbed by the stem and goes no farther.

Flexstem enthusiasts claim that it takes the danger out of places where a steep downhill ends at an abrupt angle as it meets a road or flat terrain. Normally in this situation the front wheel will dive down, throwing the rider over the handlebars. With a Flexstem, however, the front wheel is driven upward when it hits, and as it comes back down, it meets the level ground.

Flexstems come with nine bushings, each with a different degree of hardness. Riders can replace bushings for the amount of flex they desire.

A Hite-Rite (the spring mechanism shown here) allows a rider to lower the seat for tough descents without dismounting.

The Flexstem pivots downward to absorb shock to the arms.

Like the Flexstem, the new front fork suspension systems are designed to smooth out the ride. The systems, currently marketed primarily by Scott and Rock Shox, work differently: one on a spring principle, the other on a hydraulic principle.

The spring shock idea isn't new—in fact they have been used on various bike models since the 1940s. The early coil spring shocks, often a single large spring connected to the forks and the head tube, never gained wide public acceptance, but the concept never died.

Since the early 1980s, oddball mountain bikes with all manner of spring suspension systems have been introduced. However, it wasn't until Scott's Unishocks (a spring in each arm of the front fork) and Rock Shox's hydraulic (air over oil) system appeared that front-end suspension systems proved worthwhile.

Rock Shox

Rock Shox (left) replace the front forks and can be adjusted for softer or firmer suspension (below).

The tension on Scott's spring Unishocks can be adjusted, as can the air pressure on the Rock Shox. This allows the rider to set the suspension perfectly for the type of terrain or riding.

In tests, both suspension systems completely smooth out washboard road shock and allow the biker to ride directly into rocks, logs, and curbs without having to lift and lunge the front tire over them (see page 101). When the tire hits the obstacle, the wheel moves upward as the impact is absorbed by the shocks. The upward motion carries the wheel over the obstacle.

The sudden success of front suspension systems is giving rise to work on rear suspensions as well. One rear system has a coil spring surrounding an oil-filled shock; another features a large-diameter cylindrical solid elastomer shock at the junction of the bike's seatstays and seat tube, working in conjunction with a pivot-arm chainstay.

As more top-end mountain bikes come equipped with either front, rear, or dual suspension systems, it appears that sometime in the near future, they will become standard equipment on less expensive bikes, and eventually on all mountain bikes. Certainly most design efforts over the next few years will go into creating lighter-weight, maintenance-free, less expensive shock absorption systems.

Handlebar extensions are another new feature. They include bar-end additions and triathlon bars similar to those used by American road bike racer Greg LeMond during his stirring time-trial performances on his way to overall victory in the 1989 and 1990 Tours de France.

Bar-end add-ons are short cylindrical metal pieces that slide over the ends of the handlebars. They tilt slightly inward, a bit off the perpendicular, and can be canted forward as much as desired. Riders who use them swear by them— they claim that climbing is easier. The bars provide optional hand positioning that allows you to stretch your body out more on long rides and to get into a more aerodynamic tuck position when descending.

A possible downside to bar-ends is that they can catch on low-hanging branches and trailside shrubs and send the unwary rider tumbling.

Bar-ends were designed for mountain bikes. Triathlon bars were designed to let road riders stretch out and relax during a long ride. The bars are installed on the normal handlebars and have elbow pads and a forward-looping bar. There are riders who state unequivocally that triathlon bars (now made in specific mountain bike configurations) make for better downhilling and mixed-terrain riding. An equally vocal group says triathlon bars make for an unstable, dangerous ride. You be the judge, but only after you've gained enough riding experience with standard bars.

Bar-ends such as these allow for more hand positions while riding.

One noncontroversial add-on is a pump. Time was when finding a good mountain bike pump was nearly impossible. Today, while not quite a dime a dozen, there are many good, reasonably priced pumps to choose from. All come with mounts that are easily attached to the frame. I suggest placing the pump attachments on the back of the seat tube. Located there, the pump is out of the way yet handy when needed.

Many people new to mountain biking find they need a more comfortable seat. As I mentioned earlier, I recommend a good leather or synthetic seat, which with time and use will mold to your backside's contours. However, if you don't get to ride that often and need a cushier feel, look for a saddle with a built-in gel pocket. If that doesn't work, try a Spenco gel saddle cover; it adds

Two ways to attach a pump to a bike: in front of (left) or behind (right) the seat tube.

weight but it will give you a squishy, cushy seat. Never *ever* buy one of those fluffy sheepskin saddle covers advertised as perfect protection for bicycle riders. They don't work that well, and they instantly identify you as a true rube.

You're also a rube if you don't consider spending the extra money for sealed wheel hubs with quick-release mechanisms and a sealed bottom bracket. Hubs and bottom bracket, if unsealed or marginally sealed, will load up with dirt and grit over a period of time, eventually destroying the bearings and causing mechanical problems. The quick-release mechanism? Trust me. After the umpteenth time you're unable to locate the wrench to unbolt the front wheel from its fork in order to put your bike on the car-top carrier, you'll wish you'd spent the extra money to get quick-release wheel hubs. Quick-release hubs allow you to remove a wheel with a flick of the wrist. Forget carrying a wrench around to remove your wheels—go quick-release. Most bike manufacturers cover all you need to know about quick-release safety in their owner's manual.

A

Quick-release brake cables (A) and hubs (B) make removing your bike's front wheel as easy as one, two, three (C).

B

C

Mountain bikes fit differently than road bikes. To fit a road bike, you straddle the top tube and stand over it with your legs close together. There should be about an inch of clearance between the top tube and your crotch. As an example, this simple test tells me to ride a road bike with a 25-inch frame.

To fit a mountain bike, first make sure you're wearing flat-soled shoes. Straddle the bike and spread your feet out to the side, well past shoulder width. Standing thus, your crotch should have at least an inch of clearance. This test shows that my mountain bike should have a 22-inch frame.

If you fall between two frame sizes, go with the shorter frame if you plan to do most of your riding off-road and desire more control; go with the taller frame if you plan to ride mostly on paved roads.

Once you have a bicycle that fits, the two most important components to

Bike height.
A mountain bike is the right height if, when you straddle it, you can lift it only an inch or so off the ground.

fine-tune for a better ride are the saddle and the handlebars. The saddle must be at the right height, proper fore and aft position, and correct angle so that you can get the most out of each pedal stroke and thereby minimize leg fatigue.

To set your saddle height, sit on the saddle, put one pedal down with the crank arm parallel to the seat tube, and rest the heel of the foot on that pedal. Adjust the seat up and down until you are seated with just a slight bend at the knee. This is the position your leg should be in at the bottom of the pedal stroke, and signifies correct saddle height.

A saddle set too low makes for excessive leg bend and puts undue strain on your knees. A saddle set too high causes you to strain on each downward stroke, creating unnecessary leg fatigue.

The next step in saddle tuning is to make sure it's properly positioned fore and aft. Sitting too far back or too far forward inhibits smooth, fluid leg movements and pedal power. Bring the pedal from the 6 o'clock to the 3 o'clock position. The seat is in the proper fore/aft position if when you draw an imaginary line straight down from just behind your kneecap, it goes through the center of the spindle that holds the pedal to the crank arm. Many bicycle shops use a plumb line to make sure this alignment is absolutely correct.

Finally, make sure your saddle tips neither forward nor backward. A backward-slanting saddle puts too much weight over the rear wheel, which makes you feel as if you're pedaling uphill even on the flats, makes you stretch to reach the handlebars, and could cause you to slide off onto your rear tire on a steep ascent. A forward-slanting saddle puts too much of your upper body weight onto your arms. This leads to tired arms and oversteering. Women riders, however, may prefer a slight downward tip of the saddle nose for more riding comfort.

Saddle adjusted, the next important component to fine-tune is the handlebars. First, using a hacksaw or a pipe cutter, cut the ends of the bars down to shoulder width. The closer the bars are to shoulder width, the better your control over the bike. The wider the bars, the slower the steering and the more apt the bars are to catch on trailside bushes and low-hanging branches. But be careful! Cut the bars too narrow and you'll oversteer.

Cutting the handlebars down isn't as big a deal as it once was. Early production mountain bikes came with extra-wide (30-to-36-inch) "bull moose" bars. Riders made do with them until enlightenment came. Mine occurred at Crested Butte, Colorado, during a lapped mountain bike race. During each lap I'd hear bikes just ahead of me smacking their wide bars into the aspens that bordered a section of tight trail. Moments later, blam, I'd hit a tree, and recover control of the bike just in time to have a bar end hit another tree.

Saddle Height

A saddle set too low creates excessive knee bend when the pedal is at the lowest position.

A saddle set too high does not allow any knee bend at all.

A saddle at the proper position allows slight knee bend when the pedal is at the lowest position.

Handlebars.
Cut your handlebars to
shoulder width for better
bike handling.

This happened during the amateur race. When the pros rode the course, not one of them hit the trees. I noticed how much narrower their handlebars were. That night I chopped mine down to 21½ inches, and I re-rode the course the next day without hitting a tree and with superior overall bike control.

If you're buying a bike, you may be lucky. Most of today's production mountain bikes come with much narrower bars, which often don't need cutting down.

Okay, next let's look at handlebar height. The rule of thumb for most riders is to have the bars as close to level with the top of the saddle as possible. However, if you're a budding racer or a hot rider, you should set the bar height lower. On the same principle, the bigger the frame, the greater the gap between the top of the saddle and the top of the handlebars.

With the bars set, make sure the brake levers are between 35 and 45 degrees below horizontal. With them positioned thus, you should be able to

Handlebar height.
When you start out, the handlebars should be level with the saddle.

squeeze the brakes with your wrists flat. If the wrists are cocked back or forward, you lose power in your grip.

Finally, there are times when you make all the adjustments and still feel cramped or stretched out, unable to get into that comfortable basic riding position (described in Chapter 3). If you feel that your arms are too bent and your body posture too cramped, or you're too stretched out with your arms stiff and straight, no amount of saddle or handlebar adjustments will help the problem. To make the fit right, go to a good dealer and get your bike fitted with a new handlebar stem.

The stem is the piece of tubing that attaches to the head tube and, after rising several inches, juts forward at an angle. Handlebars are attached at the stem's apex. When I was a kid we called stems "goosenecks," and I still like the name. By shortening or lengthening the stem/gooseneck, you can tune your bike perfectly to your body size and arm reach.

Body Position

Here the rider's position is too cramped.

This position is too stretched out.

Now the rider's position is neither cramped nor stretched.

Changing the stem can alter your bike's fit and its ride.

THE TEST RIDE

Never buy a bike without first giving it a test ride. So what if the guy down the street swears by his Mastadon "Rock Crusher"—don't buy one until you try one. The differences between the way various bikes ride can be dramatic. It's better to test a few and find the one that rides the best within your price range. It's far better to start out with a bike you like than to buy on someone else's word and later regret that decision.

If possible, test bikes off-road, on trails—and if a shop doesn't allow test rides, go to one that does.

ALL THE RIGHT STUFF

The absolute right stuff is helmet, cycling shoes, and cycling shorts. To para-phrase the advertising slogan, "Never leave home without all three." And always buy the best you can afford. They will make your riding safer, more comfortable, and more enjoyable.

Head Case

You have to be a complete ninny not to wear a helmet. A hard fall on your head can leave you severely injured—or can even kill you.

There are three types of popular helmets on the market today: hard-shell (all plastic), ultralight EPS (Styrofoam-like material), and EPS shells covered with a thin plastic outer shell. No matter which type of helmet you finally select, it should meet the American National Standards Institute (ANSI) standard for impact protection, and ideally the even more rigid standard set by the Snell Memorial Foundation. When the salesperson tells you the helmet is ANSI and Snell approved, it's a good buy. You can double-check by looking inside the helmet for stickers from either or both groups, giving the helmet their seal of approval.

Helmets.
Basic helmet types include, from left to right, ultralight EPS foam, hard-shell plastic, and EPS foam covered with a thin plastic shell.

Good helmets come with fit pads and the Snell certification seal.

Hard, foam, and combination helmets all come with sizing pads that can be added to the lining to make the fit snugger. These helmets also all have chin straps that buckle next to your cheek or under your chin.

Not all helmets fit alike, and some models are lighter than others within the same type. Shop around, and try several helmets before you settle on the one that best fits your head shape. Never buy a too-large helmet and then try to make it fit by overloading it with fit pads. The pads are there to make a good fit a bit snugger.

I shopped until I found a light EPS foam helmet that fit a shade loosely without adding any fit pads. That way I knew I could wear the helmet over a light wool ski cap for winter riding. And with fit pads placed properly, the helmet could be made nice and snug for warm-weather riding.

I prefer EPS foam helmets because they are lightweight and because their cutouts allow air to flow through for optimal ventilation. They are a far cry from my old helmet, which produced its own humid microclimate around my head on hot days.

Other riders I know prefer hard-shell and combi helmets, reasoning that they offer far better protection. They reckon, wisely, that a few added ounces of weight are of little concern when there's risk of a head injury.

No matter which type of helmet you buy, make sure it fits properly and protects well. Always wear your helmet when you're riding. A head is a terrible thing to bash.

Mountain Feets

Let's move to the feet, where a good pair of cycling shoes can make the difference between a great and a so-so ride. Years ago a writer made the comment that if you had to choose between sneakers and a good pair of dress shoes for road riding, the dress shoes would be the better choice.

He was right. If you had a choice between those brown wingtips in the closet and your designer basketball shoes, the wingtips are it. Why? Simple: the dress shoes have stiffer soles, and it's imperative to have a stiff sole on your cycling shoe so that all your leg power is transmitted directly to the pedals. Stiff soles equal direct energy transmission; soft, flexible soles equal transmission loss and sore arches.

There are three types of mountain biking shoes to consider: lug-sole shoes, cleated shoes, and the "clipless" systems mentioned earlier. These are general categories and there are a few variations, but for the sake of clarity we'll stick with the basics.

Most lug-sole mountain biking shoes look like a cross between a sneaker and a hiking boot. In fact, hiking boots were the preferred shoe for most riders a few years ago. Today's lug-sole shoes are specially designed to fit onto pedals so that, with a toe-clip assembly, the lugs help grip the pedal on the upstroke. The lugs also help grip the ground when you're off the bike, hiking it up a steep hill or over rough ground. But the essential part of the lug-sole shoe is the rigid shank that most have, which ensures stiffness.

Lug-sole cycling shoes come in low- or high-cut styles, and the choice of cut is really a personal one. That hoary adage about a higher cut equaling more ankle support is untrue. Higher cut equaling more ankle protection is more accurate.

Lug-sole shoes are best for riders who need a versatile, comfortable shoe they can both ride and walk in. Riders who want the ultimate in perfomance must look carefully at cleated and "clipless" shoes. Basically, these are road-racing shoes adapted ever so slightly for mountain bike use. They have a streamlined appearance, are lightweight, have extremely stiff soles, and have special features such as Velcro closure flaps over the laces.

A cleated shoe has a raised cleat with a slot that fits down onto the rear wall of the pedal. With the cleat snugged down onto the pedal and the shoe's

Shoes

Lug-soled shoes come in a variety of tread patterns.

In addition, you can choose from (left to right) a "clipless" sole, a non-cleated sole, and a cleated sole.

"Clipless" soles allow you to snap the shoe's cleat into a special pedal. To release your foot, simply give it a twist.

toe held tight by the toe-clip cage and the strap over the instep, the rider gets maximum power to the pedals and maximum leg control over the bike.

"Clipless" shoes have special raised or depressed areas in the sole, receptacles that fit onto special high-tech pedal posts. The idea behind these shoes and their one-of-a-kind pedals is to offer the rider the tightest link to the bike while eliminating the often cumbersome toe-clip cage and strap assembly.

If you plan to ride your mountain bike primarily on paved roads (and according to industry figures 80 percent of mountain bike purchasers do), consider a cleated or "clipless" shoe when you purchase your bike. However, if you plan to use your bike exclusively off-road, buy a lug-sole shoe, and after you feel you have mastered most of the off-road riding techniques, consider switching to cleated or "clipless."

Short Stuff

The final must-have item is shorts. Thousands of mountain bikers ride in short shorts, running shorts, Bermuda shorts. I guarantee that these people complain about chafed legs, a sore crotch, or some other woe after every ride. Good cycling shorts reduce saddle soreness and protect your rear, crotch, and inner thighs from chafing and abrasion.

What are good cycling shorts? First, they have long, form-fitting legs that protect the inner thighs. Second, they have internal padding (chamois, synthetic chamois, polypropylene) that extends through the crotch area.

The majority of cycling shorts on the market are designed to be form-fitting and are made of body-hugging Lycra or a Lycra blend. There are good reasons for the tight fit (no excess material flapping in the breeze; padding close to the body). However, the body-hugging look is one that many people can't abide. Stand around a bike shop and you'll hear customers exclaiming as the sales clerk attempts to sell them a pair of tight Lycra shorts: "No way you're going to catch me in those. They're only for lean athletes."

It's true that once in Lycra, whatever excess flab you've been carrying around suddenly bulges out for all the world to see. However, knowing the comfort good shorts bring, you should consider them an incentive to riding yourself into shape.

For those who deem tight Lycra an absolute no-no, those clever cycling-wear manufacturers have come up with suitable alternatives. These are specially designed mountain biking shorts that look like hiking shorts with a mesh inner brief, but also include a sewn-in crotch and seat padding.

Snug-fitting shorts lined with good chamois seat padding are a must; they'll keep your legs from chafing and provide a cushier ride.

DRESSING THE PART

Historically, mountain bikers have tended to eschew traditional cycling gear. But as the sport has grown, more are wearing road-riding clothing.

After the all-important shorts, there are jerseys to consider. The traditional cycling jersey is cut long to protect your lower back and kidney area when you're hunched over in the riding position. There are pockets on the jersey's back where you can store food, tools, and even a spare tire when you ride. A jersey is nice for mountain biking, but not a necessity. The reason many mountain bikers don't use them is that they carry food and gear in saddle, frame, or fanny packs.

The other standard item worth considering carefully is gloves. The best choice, except in winter (see below), is the specially designed fingerless cycling glove with thick padding at the palm. Riders who use garden gloves, ski gloves, baseball batter's gloves, or the like will invariably complain about their hands turning numb. Part of the numbness comes from using a "death grip" on the bars and part from not having ample padding at the palm of the hand to absorb

Helmet, top, shorts, shoes, and a properly fitted bike are the basics to getting started in mountain biking.

shock. Use anything but a cycling glove and you'll find your hands coated with perspiration after even the shortest summer ride. That's why traditional cycling gloves are open at the back: they allow air to circulate around your hands and thus prevent perspiration buildup.

Winter Layers

Mountain bikes are eminently suited for riding in winter conditions—snow, slush, ice, mud—and dressing in layers is the key to bundling up for a cold-weather ride. This means wearing several layers of light clothing instead of one heavy, thick, insulative layer. You peel the layers off as you warm up and put them back on as you start to cool down. This is the way those who work and play in the cold have always dressed.

It's most important to cover the extremities—hands, feet, head—first. They are always the first parts of the body to get cold and the last to warm up.

The best winter riding gloves I've used are lightly insulated cross-country ski racing gloves. Better a lightly insulated glove, for handlebar grip, shifting, and brake lever control, than a thickly insulated alpine ski glove whose bulk inhibits hand and finger control.

If you purchase a pair of lightly lined gloves and find them a shade cold, buy a pair of polypropylene, silk, or nylon liner gloves for an extra layer of warmth. You remove the liners when your hands warm up and put them back on if your hands get cold.

Studies conducted by the U.S. Army, among others, have shown that over 50 percent of your body heat escapes through your head. Knowing that, it's obvious that with judicious use of a knit wool ski hat or special cycling cap, you can regulate your body temperature. The hat becomes the thermostat for maintaining or shedding body heat.

Put the hat on under your helmet on a cold day. When you get hot, remove the cap. Immediately you'll begin to notice that your body temperature starts to lower. Later, as you cool down, replace the hat to warm things back up.

You can keep your feet warm by wearing specially designed insulated overboots, old socks, or toe-clip covers. Most overboots are designed to be used with cleated or "clipless" shoes. (There is an opening in the boot's sole where the cleat or "clipless" receptacle pokes through to engage the pedal.) While the majority of these booties consist of a windproof outer material backed with insulative foam, there are also Neoprene models.

Some overboots don't work well with thicker lug-sole shoes—there's too little exposed sole for good pedal grip. So I devised my own overboots: I pull oversize ragg wool or cotton athletic socks over my shoes. To get good pedal-to-sole hold, I cut out a portion of the bottom of the socks. This is an inexpensive way to ensure warm feet.

Also available are windproof nylon covers that slip over the toe clips. These work surprisingly well at keeping the entire foot warm.

Getting to the Core of It

Now we move to the body's core, where proper layering is critical. The first core layer should be a synthetic underwear top. Synthetic underwear wicks, or transports, perspiration vapor away from your skin and passes it off through the material's outer layer. The result is dry material next to your skin. Among the brand names to look for in transport underwear are Medalist's Skinetics, Patagonia's Capillene, Kenyon's Toastys, Terramar's MT 3000, and from numerous suppliers, Thermax and polypropylene.

On top of the underwear comes a light insulative layer: either a wool or synthetic cycling jersey or a fleece or light wool sweater. This layer traps and holds warm air around the body.

The final layer is the windproof layer. It keeps wind out and keeps your internal heat shield intact. There are many choices in outer shell garment styles and fabrications, including nylon windbreaker-like jackets, high-tech jackets

A warm, insulating mid layer, booties, lightly lined gloves, and a ski cap are essential for cold-weather riding.

made with Gore-Tex and similar waterproof/breathable fabrics, and specially designed cycling jackets that combine panels of nylon for wind protection with a synthetic knit material for warmth. The choice is yours and usually comes down to how much money you'd like to spend.

Choices in leg coverings are far more limited. The best riding tights I've used are made of thick Lycra (a few millimeters thicker than aerobics tights material) with a layer of synthetic foam lining the front of each leg for added wind protection. These tights are warm and comfortable. They can be worn over biking shorts without the need for long underwear. If it gets too cold, I add a pair of knee-length socks under the tights for added protection.

From the Closet

Some of your regular clothes can also be used for winter riding. Long underwear, a rain jacket, a ski cap, and aerobics tights immediately come to mind. Use what you have, with the following caveats.

If you wear long underwear under cycling shorts, the underwear will chafe around the crotch. Also, as you ride, the long underwear moves one way, the outerwear tights the other. The end result is repeated stops to adjust the clothing disorder.

If you use baggy sweat pants with nylon wind pants over them for added protection, the combination inhibits leg movements and will eventually lead to a sudden, dramatic stop as a loose pant leg flaps into the chainrings.

Jeans Ban

Blue jeans are wonderful fashion wear. However, they are not good cycling wear, especially in cool, damp weather. Jeans are made of cotton denim, which absorbs and retains moisture. Get a cold, clammy layer of cotton next to your skin on a rainy ride and be prepared for an introduction to hypothermia.

RAIN COVER

Some people say they refuse to ride in the rain. If they lived in places like the rainy side of the Cascades in the Pacific Northwest, they'd either learn to ride when it's wet or abandon cycling.

There are as many ideas about what to wear for rainy-day riding as there are rainwear manufacturers. Basically, it's always a good idea to ride in a trimly

Choosing the proper rainwear is a matter of how much you are willing to sweat and how much you want to pay.

cut jacket that doesn't flap in the breeze, that has vents that allow perspiration vapor to escape, and that is designed to be wind- and rainproof.

Specially designed cycling jackets are cut short-waisted in front but have extended backs that cover you completely when you're hunched over in the riding position. Many of these jackets also have "pit-zips," underarm zippers that can be opened for ventilation as perspiration vapor builds inside the jacket.

Better-designed mountaineering and general rainwear jackets will do in a pinch, but they are heavier and more cumbersome than the specially designed cycling jackets. A better choice would be a less bulky running suit or golf rainwear jacket.

Waterproof/Breathables

Bring up rainwear and the subject invariably turns to waterproof/breathable fabrics. More precisely, to Gore-Tex, a membrane manufactured by the W. L. Gore Company, which when applied to various fabrics reportedly renders them both waterproof and breathable.

Gore-Tex has become synonymous with waterproof/breathables, but there are other companies that make equally fine products. Whatever manufacturer or product you're considering, a waterproof/breathable fabric jacket is a spendy proposition. And this can be particularly grating when, after the money has been spent, the miracle fabric doesn't live up to either advertised claims or your expectations. From my point of view, Gore-Tex and the other materials shed the rain well, are windproof, and breathe when aided by pit-zips or other vents.

Despite all the advancements in materials, however, coated nylon repels moisture better than the best of the waterproof/breathables. But it doesn't breathe a wit. So what? For a quarter of what a Gore-Tex jacket costs, you can get a rain jacket that's waterproof. Sure, it will trap perspiration and feel like a traveling sauna, but you can overcome a bit of that discomfort by making sure you're wearing light layers underneath.

Some riders feel that unless it's raining cats and dogs, there's no need for any type of rain gear. They wear light water-repellent (not waterproof) jackets over a synthetic fleece or pile sweater. If the jacket gets soaked through, the sweaters, made from water-hating fibers, can be removed, wrung free of trapped water, and put back on to provide a warm insulative layer.

I've avoided talking about rain pants because I think they're useless for cycling. I wear tights and let my legs get wet. Rain pants interfere with leg movements, get hung up in the chainrings, slide down as you pedal, and make it difficult to get off and on the saddle.

As a last note on rainwear, glasses wearers should try using a cycling cap under their helmet. The cap's bill will help keep rain off the face and specs. Also worth noting is that if your glasses start to fog up, unzip your jacket about 8 inches. Heat funneling up through the jacket's collar and onto your face is generally the culprit.

A billed bicycle cap worn under the helmet can help keep rain off your specs.

NIGHT RIDERS

If you ride at night, wear something reflective on your bike or body that car headlights can pick up. Most bikes come equipped with reflectors. They aren't enough. It isn't necessary to spend your entire budget on a fancy jacket with reflective panels when you can buy an inexpensive reflective sash or vest that you can slip on over your riding clothes. Both make a bold "night rider" fashion statement.

Also get a light. The best are battery-operated models that throw off a good beam. If you ride through the winter, install your light in October in preparation for the dark months ahead, and remove it in April when the days get longer.

If a light seems impractical, purchase a headlamp that can be attached to your helmet. There are several superb lightweight battery-operated models on the market.

Lights.
If you want to ride your mountain bike at night, two typical options are either of these handlebar lights (left), or a light mounted on a rear seatstay (right).

THE EYES HAVE IT

A few years ago sport glasses became a big fad. Credit goes to Oakley for starting the craze with their "Blades" glasses. As fashionable as those and other sport glasses have become, they also serve the practical purpose of saving eyes.

In no other sport is the use of lightweight, strong, unbreakable glasses more important than in mountain biking. Fat knobby tires throw up stones, and getting hit with one between the eyes could prove disastrous—remember Goliath?

Protect your eyes from flying stones, wind, and the effects of ultraviolet light with a pair of UV-resistant, shatterproof sport glasses. They're worth every cent.

Sunglasses.
The bigger the shades, the better the protection from sun and flying stones. To protect your face and eyes in case of falls, always choose shatterproof glasses.

BASIC BAGS

Because so many mountain bikers truly get away from it all, numerous carry bags have been designed to haul necessities along. Later we'll get into touring bags for extended trips; here we'll discuss basic bags—bags for day tripping.

Among the small, indispensible carry bags is the tool/repair kit that is attached to and fits under the bike saddle. In this compact, out-of-the-way bag you can keep all the tools and repair materials you might need on a ride.

There are also handlebar bags designed to hold lunch, maps, and extra clothing. A wire frame is attached to the handlebars and then the bag is inserted into the frame. Many have a clear plastic pocket in the top, into which you can insert a map for quick checks of your route as you ride.

There are large bags that attach to the rear of the saddle, if your saddle has metal eyelets that accept the pack's holding straps. One of the more interesting bag designs is a thin model that fits into the center of the bike's frame and is held to it by straps over the top tube and around the seat and head tubes. It holds enough for a day tour, does not interfere with riding movements, and is easily removed if you want to take the bag with you. (These modern inside-the-frame bags are similar to the containers used by the Army's Twenty-fifth Infantry bicycle troops in the 1890s. The Twenty-fifth's metal containers nestled into the frame, carried tools and rations, and when removed could be broken down to form cookwear and utensil sets.)

There are riders who like to carry just about as much as the soldiers did in the old Twenty-fifth. For them, the best general carryall is the metal rear rack. This rack can be outfitted with a variety of bags, from fabric models with rigid frames that fit on top of the rack to saddlebag panniers that straddle the frame. There are also open, box-like wire mesh carriers that attach to the sides of a rear rack and are perfect for carrying packages on shopping trips.

The rear rack is a worldwide standard. When I was in Korea, I marveled at the things local deliverymen managed to pile on their bike racks. It was not unusual to see a television set, a small under-the-counter refrigerator, and a bedside table all tied onto a bicycle's rear rack. Not only were the loads impressive, so were the bungee cords used to hold them in place—veritable anacondas in comparison to the short "snakes" standard in the U.S.

I marveled more recently at a Scottish forester whose rear bicycle rack was loaded down with two pruning saws, a chain saw, and a bag of miscellaneous tools. He rode, he told me, from job to job, and a fitter forester I doubt I'll ever see!

Fitting a rear rack to your mountain bike requires eyelets on the rear

An underseat tool/repair bag is a must on any ride.

This contemporary bag is a soft version of the metal frame carrier used by the Twenty-fifth Bicycle Corps in the 1890s.

The rear rack.
A rear rack is perfect for carrying such items as books (left) or, with the help of a carry bag, groceries (right).

The fanny pack is still the mountain bike rider's most versatile carryall.

seatstays. The rack's frame legs are held by screws through the eyelets. It's a good idea to make sure your bike has the proper eyelets if you plan to add a rack. And if you plan to ride when it's wet, you can buy a plastic cover that snaps over the rack's top, which will help keep mud from splashing up onto your backside.

Moving from the back to the front of the bike, a front rack can be attached, again via eyelets, at the fork dropouts. The rack is also secured, with the aid of a bracket, to the head tube. Again there are a variety of bags you can attach to the front rack, from box-like bags that ride on top of the rack to saddlebag panniers that lie over it.

For tourers who don't like racks or bags on their bikes, the best carry bag is the fanny pack. A few years ago, the term fanny pack meant a fairly large pack that could handle all the tools required on a day trip, plus a thin jacket and maybe a pair of extra gloves. Today there are fanny packs of every size and description. There is no one best size or type for mountain biking. You'll just have to make your own choice.

For warm-weather riding I use a small fanny pack designed to hold cross-country ski waxes. If I think the weather might turn sour, I tie a rain jacket around my waist.

For cold-weather riding I use a larger fanny pack that accommodates as much gear as a daypack. There is a new generation of fanny packs that expand, with the unfolding of a top extension, into large carryalls. These also work well for cycling.

The fanny pack makes sense for mountain biking because it doesn't interfere with riding movements, can be swung around to your stomach so you can retrieve something while riding, and will cushion a fall on the back. Conversely, a daypack is cumbersome, overheats your back, and requires a full stop and removal from the shoulders to get to its contents. I say, stick with the fanny pack for your day-tripping bag.

3

Basic Riding Techniques

In the basic riding position you should be slightly hunched over and arching your back comfortably, without strain. Your hands should have a firm hold (not a "death grip") on the handlebars, and your arms should be bent comfortably at the elbows. Your head is up and you're looking ahead.

That said, it might be necessary to fine-tune your seat and/or handlebar position if you are either too cramped or too stretched out on your bike. You're too cramped if your knees come close to contacting the handlebars on pedal upstrokes and you're forced into a more upright sitting position. Conversely, you're too stretched out if you feel you have to reach for the handlebars and if your back, rather than being slightly arched, is flat, almost parallel with the bike's top tube.

In such cases, a simple switch of the handlebar stem will alleviate the problem. Since stems come in an array of different heights, forward extension lengths, and extension angles, it is possible, with the aid of a qualified bicycle specialty shop mechanic or salesperson, to move the handlebars out farther to uncramp your position or bring the bars in closer to switch you from a stretched-out to a more upright position.

If you have an older mountain bike with the upright bars that were popular a few years back (they're bent so that they sweep upward), another possible change is to switch to flat bars. Upright bars put you in an overly upright riding position; flat bars will allow you to get that proper hunch in the back.

Before challenging the backcountry, do some road riding to get a feel for your mountain bike: how it shifts, how it reacts when you pedal up a short hill sitting down and using low gears versus riding that same hill standing up and using higher gears, how the bike handles at low and high speeds. Think about cornering and leaning the bike in the direction of the turn while your body stays

79

Proper body position is the key to learning riding basics quickly.

upright. A little leaning practice will pay large dividends later on during your off-road rides.

PEDAL POWER

Every time I see a mountain bike rider doing the "crank and coast," I want stop him and offer a short lecture on pedaling efficiency. A crank-and-coast rider pedals furiously for ten revolutions, then coasts, cranks and coasts, cranks and coasts. Momentum gained during each crank phase is lost during each coast phase, making this an inefficient and tiring technique.

The most efficient way to pedal is to keep the momentum continuous and to adjust that momentum by gearing up or down as the terrain demands. The key to continuous pedaling is using a complete pedal stroke. That means pushing down on the pedals and pulling up to complete each revolution of the crank arm. As I discussed earlier, the ability to accomplish a complete and powerful pedal revolution lies in having the right shoes and having a snug shoe-to-pedal link.

The idea is to keep the legs moving and the momentum at a sustained level. That level can vary from low gear "spinning," when your legs move rapidly against little resistance (good for warming up and for ascending long, arduous hills) to pedaling against the hardest resistance possible for all-out speed on the flats or downhill.

When pedaling, keep your legs moving throughout the entire revolution and try to maintain a steady momentum.

Changing gears may seem a bit mysterious when you first ride your new mountain bike, but after a time it becomes second nature. The most important thing about shifting is anticipation. Once you've mastered the basics of shifting during road tests, it's time to fine-tune those skills on your back-roads rides.

Simply stated, the left shifter moves the chain among the three chainrings; the right shifter moves the chain up and down the gears on the rear wheel. The two shifters work together to make your pedaling most efficient.

Most mountain bikes come with three chainrings: the large ring (which I call the power ring), the middle ring (the general-purpose ring), and the small ring (the help-me-up ring).

The middle ring is the one used for most flat and gradual up- and downhill pedaling. You pedal along with the chain on the middle ring and flick your right thumb shifter to get into a gear with exactly the right amount of resistance. (A warning here: For the sake of your knees and legs, don't try to be a hero and push against the heaviest resistance. Find a resistance level that makes the legs work but without constant stress.)

Say you come to a long downhill or a nice flat section, and there's absolutely no resistance when you pedal along in the middle chainring position. This is the time to shift and move the chain onto the large ring. Now adjust the right shifter to fine-tune the resistance level. As the chain rolls over the larger ring, resistance is greater and you can really pour on the power.

(Another warning: Be sure you're well warmed up before making a big gear push. Hitting the big gears hard early in a ride, or early in the riding season, can severely strain your knees.)

The small chainring is used for uphill riding—any uphill you can't make on the middle chainring or don't care to force. On the small ring, the chain spins through quickly, and by adjusting the right shifter you can fine-tune the exact amount of resistance you want for climbing the hill.

Those are the basics, and frankly they're all a rider needs to know to get started. The more you ride, the more shifting becomes a reflex.

There is one valuable technical point, though: Your gearing works most effectively when the chain forms a relatively straight line between the chainring and the rear gear cluster. To see what I mean, shift onto the large chainring. You'll notice that when you shift the rear gears into their highest position (lowest gear), the chain is at an oblique angle as it travels from front to rear. Now shift the rear gears down, and see how the chain shifts position as you shift and soon will travel in a straighter path from chainring to gear cluster. A straight-traveling chain equals efficiency.

This simple test also shows that the large chainring works more efficiently in concert with the smaller rear gears. A test with the small ring would show that the larger rear gears (greater number of teeth) mesh better for a straighter line between chainring and gear cluster.

ANTICIPATION

Mountain bike racing's first genuine hero was Joe Murray, a quiet, unassuming Marin County rider. Murray was exceptionally adept at maintaining momentum throughout a race. I recall a professional rider evaluating Murray's strengths in these words: "He doesn't climb exceptionally well, he's an okay descender, but nobody rides rolling terrain better. Joe's anticipation is incredible."

Anticipating terrain changes and changing gears, leg speed, and riding position for them made Joe Murray virtually unbeatable for several years. This practice also makes the difference between struggling through a ride and flowing through it. Anticipation allows you to carry speed—fast or slow—through changes in terrain rather than slowing to a near halt, shifting gears, and then overexerting to regain momentum.

Before giving an example, let's clarify "up" and "down" in shifting. Many riders refer to up or down shifts according to the way the chain moves on the rear gear cluster: up to a larger cog or down to a smaller cog. Other riders say "up" when they mean getting into a higher gear (smaller cog) and "down" when they shift into a lower gear (larger cog). For simplicity's sake, we'll use "up" and "down" to indicate the way the chain moves from the middle of the

When you're riding, anticipation is everything—be alert for whatever comes next.

A   B   C

Oops!
Trying to conquer an uphill in too big a gear usually ends like this: grunt (A), strain (B), step off (C).

gear cluster: *up* to the larger cogs (lower gears) and *down* to the smaller cogs (higher gears).

Now here's an example: You come to a short, easy downhill—not very steep. You could coast this hill, but looking ahead you see a short, gradual uphill. Instead of coasting, you shift down a couple of gears (you're on the middle chainring) and push for a bit more speed. You pedal through the outrun of the downhill, across the flat, and as the uphill starts, you shift up, anticipating the climb. You keep shifting as the angle of the hill increases. As you crest the hill, you shift down for more resistance in order to keep the momentum going and to start rebuilding speed.

Steeper hills require shifting off the middle ring to the small ring and using special riding techniques that we'll cover later. For now, the important lesson is to anticipate gear changes and learn to execute them so that your bike keeps moving.

What happens if you lose momentum? A typical scenario goes like this: The rider coasts that downhill we just described, enjoying the rest, until the bike's momentum has almost stopped. Too late, he realizes that it's time to shift. He shifts, and by the time the shifting is completed the bike has started to wobble and he is fighting to control it. If he wins control, it has taken a major output of energy; if he loses control, he topples over. This scenario is avoidable if you anticipate those gear changes and smooth out your ride!

4

Getting Up

Psychologically, uphills are the hardest part of any ride. People either love uphills or hate them. The hate group is far larger, but I'm an uphill lover. There's nothing like a steep, long, tricky uphill to test your riding skills and mental resolve.

A bit of bluster there? No, just the fact that most tall, skinny geeks like myself excel in the ups rather than the downs, where being built closer to the ground is an advantage.

There are many ways to climb a hill—and to climb them with control, minimal exertion, and pleasure.

GETTING UP BY STAYING DOWN

Most short, slightly inclined hills are best climbed by staying firmly seated in the saddle, gearing up, and spinning along. "Spinning" refers to the rapid leg movement when you pedal against low resistance. Practicing spinning can help you keep your legs loose and strong over a long ride.

When you approach a low-angled short hill, sit tight, shift up, and pedal on through. There's really no need to change your body position or to drop off the middle chainring. That's why you have that rear gear cluster. Just shift up a couple of gears and proceed.

If the angle of the hill steepens, you have to make some adjustments. First, you've got to anticipate the steeper incline and shift to the small chainring. Spinning along in the small ring, you shift gears up or down to get the right amount of resistance.

All goes well until the hill steepens just a bit more and your front tire starts

85

Master the right techniques and those dreaded uphills won't be so dreadful.

Getting up by staying down means spinning in a low gear and leaning forward.

to lift off the ground. Now you're fighting for control over the bike. You grip the handlebars tighter, which only makes the front wheel lift up more. You pull back, and the wheel comes up higher. Soon all things conspire for a fall.

In hill climbing, remember: (1) never get a "death grip" on your handlebars, and (2) as the steepness of the hill increases, your forward lean should increase.

A "death grip" creates a backward pull on the bars that starts to bring the front wheel up off the ground. If you stay in the normal riding position and the hill's incline steepens, your body weight naturally shifts to the rear wheel. This shift, along with the "death grip" pull, brings the front tire up off the ground. By leaning forward more and pushing against the handlebars, weight and force are more evenly distributed over the bike for better climbing and traction.

OUT OF THE SADDLE

Eventually the hill will be too steep to ride sitting down. You have to get up out of the saddle. If you're new to bicycle riding, spend a few hours on paved roads, getting used to being up and out of the saddle and experiencing how the bike tips from side to side with each pedal stroke.

When you're out of the saddle the bike does tip, so it's important again not to have a "death grip" on the handlebars. Why? Because an iron grip will either inhibit natural side-to-side movement or will yank the bike too far over as it tips. The latter case will cause a sideways fall.

When you stand out of the saddle, try to achieve a delicate balance of your weight on the pedals, handlebars, and front and rear wheels. Putting too much weight on your arms and leaning too far forward often results in a rear-wheel spinout. To compensate, you might overshift so that more body weight is borne by your legs. This move, in combination with a slight backward lean to accomplish it, will result in the front wheel hopping up off the ground.

So what to do? Ride a lot. Sounds awfully pat and smart, doesn't it, but the fact is that the more you ride, the more you'll begin to understand how you need to move your body back and forth to make your bike climb properly.

When you're out of the saddle, climbing, and the rear wheel starts to spin out, shift your weight back just a bit (the best way is to jut your rear aft) and you'll regain tire purchase. Later, if the front wheel starts to pop up off the ground, hunch forward more and put more pressure on your arms to make the front end stay down.

These movements are subtle and require time to master. However, the general rule of thumb is to keep your weight evenly distributed between arms and legs while you lean fore or aft to compensate for spinouts or wheel lifts.

Out of the saddle, the rider balances his weight fore and aft over the bike.

THE POUNCE

All hail Joe Murray once again, for giving a name to a superb uphill technique: the pounce. What Murray found as a racer, and later most of us discovered through trial and error, was that the position midway between being completely out of the saddle and staying put in it is perfect for difficult ascents. Murray labeled it The Pounce because it makes you look like a cheetah about to spring for the kill.

In the pounce position, your rear is just off the saddle and you're hunched far forward with your arms sharply bent, elbows well out to the side. It's a rock-solid position that allows you to subtly shift your weight fore and aft.

The pounce works. With it you maintain a lower, more stable center of gravity for superior bike control. Ready to pounce, you're like a sprinter coming out of the blocks—low, compact, and forceful.

Mountain biking's first top racer and master pouncer, Joe Murray.

When performing the Pounce, your weight should be forward, your rear just off the saddle, as if you're about to spring for the kill.

The best technique for long hills is a combination of in- and out-of-saddle riding: in for the overall grunt work, out for the steep sections and for overcoming obstacles. It's important to practice moving in and out of the saddle on long uphills to see which position works better and when.

Uphill body movement.
In this sequence, note how the rider's body shifts fore and aft to keep the bike under control on the uphill.

WHEN GRANNY HELPS

There are days when every hill seems too steep; there are hills that even the best riders have trouble with. These are times for those extra-small granny-gear chainrings that allow you to spin up the steepest of hills.

A bike shop owner and expert rider I know thinks a 24-tooth chainring should be installed as the standard small ring on all mountain bikes. With this small chainring and a rear gear cluster balanced in favor of larger low gears, you can granny up almost any hill.

There's an ultra-small fourth chainring called the Mountain Tamer Quad on the market. It's a 21-tooth affair, and one of my riding companions swears by it. However, he cautions that it sometimes takes some adaptation to get a Tamer to fit your bike. Other Mountain Tamer fans warn that they are difficult to shift onto and will not work with some of the derailleurs on the market. What to do? For now, stick with a smaller third ring (24-tooth, ideally), and only if you have continued climbing problems add a fourth ring.

WALKING THAT DOG

The time will come when you surrender and say, "I can't ride up this hill, no matter what!" It's push or carry time.

If the terrain isn't too rough or the hill too steep, pushing your bike uphill is easier and less tiring than carrying. For best results, grab the rear of the saddle in one hand, the top of the handlebar stem in the other (to keep the wheel from veering off to one side or the other), lean forward so that most of your weight is on the arm holding the stem—and push. Make long strides, not itty bitty steps, that reach up the hill.

If the hill is too steep and too rutted, rocky, or muddy for a decent push, it's time for a carry. Let's go through the carry basics for a right-handed person; reverse them if you're a lefty.

For the big push, grasp the handlebar with one hand, the rear of the seat with the other, and stride up the hill.

Grab the bike's top tube with your right hand placed underneath it, palm up. Grasp the handlebars with your left hand. Now lift the bike up onto your right shoulder and move the frame forward until the junction of the top tube and the seat tube is nestled against the back of your shoulder. After the bike is comfortably set on your shoulder, keep your right hand on the top tube. The left hand keeps the front wheel from flopping from side to side and tips the bike's front end up or down for better balance.

Another technique is to extend the right arm forward, once the bike is set on your right shoulder, and grip the top of the handlebar stem with your right hand. Your left arm can then swing freely to the side to act as a counterbalance.

Carrying can be a literal pain in the neck, as well as in the shoulder and arm. Shift the bike from shoulder to shoulder if it's a long carry. If you expect to be carrying your bike often, buy a carrying pad, which fits into the angle at the junction of the top and seat tubes.

The uphill carry.
There are two efficient ways to carry a bike uphill. Method A (left) gives you control over your bike; method B (right) is better for rougher terrain where you need a free arm for balance.

A

B

5

Downhills

It takes a lot of riding time and skills work to erase downhill doubts. The work is worth it because there's no greater fun than cruising downhill under control.

The basic body position for descents is up and out of the saddle, holding the saddle with your thighs, and with about 90 percent of your weight on your feet. The pedals are parallel, at the 3 and 9 o'clock positions. Your grip on the handlebars is relaxed; your arms are loose and bent easily at the elbows. Your head is up, with your eyes focusing at least 5 yards ahead down the trail. This is called "riding the pegs," a term borrowed from off-road motorcyclists, who use the same out-of-the-seat position when riding over rough terrain and most downhills.

There are two basic ways to ride the pegs. The first is more upright, with your legs straighter and your rear high up off the saddle. This is a good technique for low speeds downhill, over easier terrain, and for overcoming trail obstacles on the flats.

The second position is lower. The legs are slightly more bent, the upper body is more hunched over, and the rear is up a few inches off the saddle.

In both positions the legs act as shock absorbers. Good riders, copying motorcyclists, keep their arms loose, pumping them back and forth, up and down, with every bump. The upper body moves in conjunction with the arms, bending forward to absorb a shock and swaying back slightly after it has passed.

Again, anticipation is important. You have to be alert so you can grip the handlebars just a bit tighter and brace the legs before impact.

93

The recipe for a great downhill? Steep terrain and equal measures of fear, adrenalin, intensity, and technique.

Riding the Pegs

There are two basic ways to ride the pegs: high (left), when making slow descents, and low (below), when moving faster.

As is generally the case in mountain biking, when taking downhills, anticipation is everything. (Note the rider's arm position—flexed to absorb unexpected bumps and jolts.)

THE REAR DROP

When the hills get steeper and rougher, one of the best ways to maintain control is to move your rear off the saddle and down toward the rear wheel. (You'll know you've gone too far if your shorts start to rub rubber.) You're in the right position if your waist is just an inch or so above the rear of the saddle. This position is known among mountain bikers as the rear drop.

The rear drop helps when the going gets steep and bumpy, the rear wheel starts to bounce around wildy, and it's hard to get a good grip on the brake levers. By dropping back off the saddle, you put weight on the rear wheel to calm it down. You also take weight off your arms as you stretch to the rear drop position, allowing for better leverage on the brake levers.

To keep your rear wheel from fishtailing on a downhill, drop your backside aft, as shown here.

Paul Thomasberg—World Mountain Bike Championship downhill bronze medalist—attacks a downhill in a tuck.

THE TUCK

Smooth, fast downhills beg to be taken with speed. The safest position for speedy descents is the tuck. Stay down in your saddle, but shift your rear back so that it rests on the back of the saddle. Hunch low so that your back is parallel to the top tube, and bend your arms so that the elbows flare to the side. Tuck your head down between your arms, raising it every so often to look ahead for obstacles and changes of direction.

Try to form a tight airfoil. You'll notice that when you lift your head up from its position between the arms, the wind resistance immediately increases. Knowing this, you'll find that rather than using your brakes alone to stop, you can sit upright in the saddle and let the wind resistance help slow you down. It works!

GRAVITY CHECK

There's no question that being down closer to the ground means a safer descent. An easy way to make sure you stay low is to lower your seat at the top of the hill. That's right, dismount and lower the seat.

With the seat down, when you get up to ride the pegs and grip the seat with your thighs, you'll be in a much lower body position, thereby maintaining a lower center of gravity.

If you can't abide stopping to lower your seat at the top of the hill or raise it back up at the bottom, use a Hite-Rite, described on page 45. This simple spring device, which is attached to the seat post's quick-release, lets you raise and lower the seat without stopping. When you want to lower your seat, reach down and open the quick-release. The seat will slide down under your body weight. When it's as far down as you like, shut the quick-release to hold the position. At the bottom of the hill, unlatch the quick-release, and while standing on the pedals, allow the spring to uncoil, bringing the seat back up to its preset normal height. Hite-Rites add weight to the bike but are an invaluable aid to riders who prefer roller-coaster-like hill and mountain rides and don't want to waste time or lose momentum by stopping to change their saddle's height.

PEDALS PARALLEL

As I mentioned earlier, make your descent with your pedals parallel, at the 3 and 9 o'clock positions—the same as when you're riding the pegs. If you ride with one pedal down and one up, you're going to hit a rock with the down pedal and the bike will careen out of control.

Pedals parallel, pro rider Max Jones hurtles downhill.

KEEP THE MO

The worst mistake you can make is to slow way down. Keep the momentum going forward. To get technical for a moment: revolving wheels provide a gyroscopic effect, meaning that the faster they rotate, the more the bike continues to maintain its line. Braking robs you of this gyro effect.

With speed you roll over obstacles; without speed you roll into obstacles and stop or fall.

BRAKING

The right-hand brake lever controls the rear brake; the left one controls the front brake. Most riders use the rear brake for 75 percent or more of their braking needs. However, on downhills it's imperative to use both front and rear brakes equally. The key is to pump them, never locking either one up completely. Squeeze and let off, squeeze and let off, until you've slowed to a speed you feel comfortable with.

That old axiom "If you use the front brake, you'll get tossed over the handlebars and onto your nose" applies only if you use the front brake exclusively and lock it up.

Rounding a curve.
When rounding a curve while traveling downhill, lean the bike into the curve as shown and point your knees, particularly the inside one, in the direction you wish to turn.

A

B

C

TURNS

Reporting on a mountain bike race, a breathless radio correspondent expressed amazement at how the racers leaned rather than steered their bikes through corners. Gee whiz! If you steer through a corner (turn the handlebars in the direction of the turn), eventually you'll oversteer and crash. Or the tire will dig into loose dirt or sand, or slide out from under you on loose gravel, and you'll crash.

Crashes we don't need. Smooth corners we do. To accomplish them, keep the handlebars fixed and lean the bike in the direction of the turn. Keep your upper body erect and point your knees in the direction of the turn. As you come out of the turn, bring the bike back upright and reset your knees straight ahead.

Braking Turns

Brake before the turn, not halfway through it. Anticipate the upcoming turn, pump the brakes equally to slow down, lean into the curve, and as you start cornering, release the brakes to glide through.

Or you can begin pedaling when you release the brakes, provided, of course, that the route is relatively smooth and there's little chance of your pedals hitting rocks.

D

E

LEVER GRIP

Perhaps the most-asked question about downhill riding is "How can I keep a grip on the handlebars and use the brakes at the same time?" It's easy once you get used to it. The palm of your hand is pressed against the handlebar grips, and your thumb is hooked under the grip. So you have four fingers free to grasp the brake levers.

Most people like the four-finger grip and therefore prefer long brake levers. However, many experienced riders prefer the new shorter brake levers that are operated exclusively with the index and middle fingers.

I use long levers, keeping the index and middle fingers of both hands loosely on them at the start of any descent, and I use those fingers exclusively if all goes well. If things get rough, I get all four fingers on the levers, ready for action.

HOPSTACLES

There comes a time in downhill riding, and uphills as well, when those rocks, logs, roots, and ruts you've been swerving around have to be met head on. For this you have to learn how to "hop" over the obstacles.

Anticipation is everything. As you approach a small boulder or log, get up on the pegs, get a firm grip on the handlebars, and just as you're about to hit, pull up sharply on the bars. Pulling lifts the front wheel up off the ground, and it will either clear the obstacle or roll over it. With experience you'll be able to gauge just how much oomph is needed to pull up over different-size obstacles.

The lift and lunge.
To perform the lift and lunge, approach the low obstacle at speed (A). Just as the front wheel nears the obstacle, lift up vigorously. Then, with a bit of strong forward body thrust, lunge the bike over (B, C).

A

With larger rocks and logs, once the front wheel has cleared or rolled over, rock your upper body forward and push on the handlebars to give added forward momentum; this brings the rear wheel over the obstacle. This move is called the "lift and lunge." If you fail to make the lunge, the bike may lose speed, resulting in the rear wheel bashing into the obstacle and the bike stopping dead.

Now to ruts. The best way to pass over a rut is with a basic bunny hop. The bunny hop is that maneuver adored by all pre-adolescent boys on their BMX bikes—that quick move that brings both wheels up off the ground. The bike momemtarily flies through the air, inches off the ground, then plops back down to terra firma.

To bunny hop properly, simultaneously pull up on the handlebars and pull up your legs. It's harder than it sounds, particularly the leg part. But the result of quickly pulling your legs and arms upward will be that the front and rear wheels lift off the ground enough so you'll sail over the rut. Using toe clips or "clipless" systems is essential in order to make the upward leg retraction that helps lift the rear wheel off the ground.

Now I'd be lying if I told you that with experience, most bunny hops are flawlessly executed. Most hops favor the bike's front wheel: instead of getting both wheels a few inches off the ground, you get the front wheel up high and the rear wheel just a few inches up. This results in the rear wheel hitting a bit of the rut as you traverse it, but better that than the front wheel diving headlong into the rut and you flying over the handlebars. That slight jolt as the rear wheel bumps down into the rut is a small price to pay for clearing it safely.

B

C

The Bunny Hop

Here, Paul Thomasberg takes the same obstacle using the bunny-hop technique. He approaches the obstacle at speed.

As his front wheel nears the obstacle, he pulls up even more vigorously and unweights. The bike's wheels leave the ground.

He completes the hop with a forward lunge, keeping his arms flexed to reduce the shock of the landing, his pedals parallel, and his rear off the seat.

Riding downhill on an obstacle-strewn trail requires not only precise maneuvering and quick reactions, it also requires picking the best line through the obstacles, the line that's fast and safe. Attacking a tough downhill is like running a difficult rapid in a kayak or canoe—you have to be aware of what's ahead and pick a route that avoids the dangers.

Just like the kayaker or canoeist "reading" easy rapids from his boat, so the mountain biker can, on easy downhills, "read" the lay of the land by looking ahead down the trail. Again, anticipation is key. Learning to "read" comes with experience, but no matter how easy a trail may appear, never take your eyes off what's coming up, and always pick a route you feel will be hazard-free.

There are times when a particularly difficult route requires scouting. Kayakers and canoeists will stop at the top of an unknown or difficult rapid and scout it from the shore. After picking a suitable safe line through the rapid,

When faced with a tough downhill, stop, look, and carefully pick the route you will take.

they paddle through. The same situation occurs in mountain biking when everyone stops, looks over a section of steep trail or open downhill, and decides what line they'll take. Choose wisely and don't be the one who later says, "I took a horrible line. It was full of huge ruts. You had the right line—it looked clean except for a few big rocks." Learn to "read" the terrain, trail, and hill in order to pick a good line.

WHEN FAST IS SAFE
AND NOT SAFE

I suspect, based on personal crash history, that the majority of falls on downhills occur at slow speeds. It's important to maintain speed to ride over and through obstacles. The amount of speed you carry is directly proportionate to the control you have over the bike. Great riders will tear down a hill that novice riders might timidly roll down. It is better to attack a downhill a notch or two below "redline," or "going over the edge," than to tiptoe down it at moderate speed.

Of course variations in terrain, soil type, weather, body condition, and other factors will dictate speed on any given day. That logging trail that can be taken at top speed on a dry day will require a great deal of caution on a wet day when the soil is soggy, the trail scarred with runoff ruts.

The bottom line on speed is control. Ride near to the limit of control and back off a bit. That's the best speed groove to be in.

The controlled bailout.

There are times when bailing out of a radical downhill is the better part of valor. To perform a controlled bailout, start by easing your rear aft and off the saddle, and grasp the saddle horn with one hand (A). Using the bike for stability, dismount off the back, bringing your other

A

B

GREAT ESCAPES

There comes a time in downhill riding when you need to abandon your bike. Mountain bikes can take a lot more punishment than your body can, so when the time comes to walk away, do so with pleasure.

Let's say you're heading down a steep, rocky grade. Suddenly you're out of control and a fall is imminent. Now's the time to quickly remove one foot from its toe clip (or snap it out of the clipless system pedal) and slide your rear to the back of the saddle. The latter is easy because you're probably riding back there to begin with.

Then, with a fast move, let go of the handlebars, step onto the ground with the foot that's out of the clips, bring the other foot out of its clip to the ground, and as you come off the bike grab its seat post with one hand. Remember to bend your legs and dig your heels in to stop the momentum. This dismount saves you and the bike. However, at high speeds it may be impossible to grab the seat post—in that case, let the bike go and save your skin.

Let's put a few more good-size rocks on the trail you just rode. It's hard to lift the front wheel over them. Bam! You hit one, and like an angry rodeo bronco, your bike rears up on its front wheel and starts to send you up over the handlebars.

This is the time not to panic but to execute a "walkover." Walking over simply means timing it so that when your bike is perpendicular to the ground, you let go of the handlebars, step out of the toe clips/pedals, and take a giant step (or steps) over the bars and away from the bike. As you trot down the hill, the bike crashes to the ground behind you.

hand back to the saddle and moving your legs quickly to one side of the rear wheel (B, C). Holding on to the saddle with one hand, run alongside the bike until you can bring both it and yourself to a stop (D).

C

D

A   B

Losing control.
When taking downhills, control is everything. Here the rider loses control—and pays for it dearly.

Walkovers work, are surprisingly easy to perform (they almost come naturally), and are best done at low and moderate speeds. At high speed, it's often hard to react fast enough to walk away from a bucking bike.

Experienced riders don't practice walkovers, they simply are prepared to make a couple every year. I know I'll be over the front at least half a dozen times annually, so I always loosen my toe clips before any tough downhill so that if I need to walk over, my feet won't be fixed firmly to the pedals.

C

D

6

Ground Control

Nothing's assured in mountain bike riding. A trail that rode easily yesterday is difficult today. You may have mastered riding in the Rockies, but that doesn't mean you're going to be a hotshot on Appalachian mountain trails, the Southwest's slickrock, or the volcanic dust and lava of the Pacific Northwest.

I thought I'd mastered the art of bike handling. Then I left the comforts of the Oregon high desert for a mountain biking vacation in Vermont, and suddenly I was struggling with bike control. After riding on open rocky, sandy roads and trails in Oregon, in Vermont I was confronted with tight muddy trails crisscrossed with exposed, slick, thick tree roots. It was a new experience, and I had to learn how to cope with it or suffer a disastrous vacation.

SOGGY AND ROOTY

There's only one tip I have for mud riding, and that is *persevere*. Don't shift into a high gear and try to force your bike through the mud. Force to the rear wheel will only dig it deeper into the muck. Keep a steady pace, spinning along in a low gear. Also keep a shade more weight on the handlebars to compress the mud with your front tire, so that when the rear tire rolls through, it has the chance of improved purchase. Once free of the mud, squeeze and release both brake levers several times to clear mud off the wheel rims.

Now to those gnarly roots. A 5-inch-thick exposed root lying across a trail at an oblique angle doesn't sound too scary, but it can be one tough obstacle. The problem I have with roots is that after I've lifted the front wheel over them, my rear wheel inevitably slides along the front or top of the root, pitching the bike over sideways.

109

Just as in downhills, climbing every mountain and fording every stream is more fun when you have the bike under control.

Exposed roots and logs.
When negotiating an exposed root or
log, make your angle of attack as
nearly perpendicular to it as possible
(A) before making your lift and lunge
over (B, C).

A

Even on dry days, roots seem slippery. You have to be prepared to maneuver your bike in a way that enlarges the angle between the front wheel and the
root. Hitting the root at a 90-degree angle is safer than hitting it at a 30- or
60-degree angle.

As you approach the root, speed up slightly, pull the front wheel up over
the root, and then lunge your upper body forward for added momentum to
bring the rear wheel up and over.

On a truly rooty trail, you make one lift-and-lunge move after another. The
mental tension mounts with each crossing, and your arms start to turn to jelly
from the lifting and the shock of the impact. Try to persevere, as it's better to
have frayed nerves and numb arms than to suffer a big bruise on your leg from
a fall.

The lift-and-lunge technique applies equally well on uphills. However, it's
important to maintain momentum because at slow climbing speeds the rear
wheel is more likely to stop when it hits a root, and as you pedal for the power
to bring it over, it spins out, sending you sprawling.

B

C

VOLCANO LAND

Where I live, when we're not riding relatively smooth logging roads we're fighting our way through lava rubble, thick sand, and that finely crushed pumice we call "moon dust."

Volcanic rock is sharp-edged rock, and riding trails littered with it require the lift-and-lunge and a bit more. The extra technique is "angling," constantly moving the bike around small rocks and obstacles. To angle around something, you lean the bike quickly left or right, just as you would around a corner. The difference here is that the bike is traveling in a straight line and the lean angles it just enough to skim past trouble.

Sand is double trouble. If you hit sand, get in a low gear and spin along. Don't try to get manly and power your way through—you'll dig yourself into a hole. (See my comments on mud!)

Hitting sand at the end of a fast downhill can be tricky. If you hit sand at speed, the front wheel tends to dive down into it. A wheel dive can send you

Riding through lava rock is tough, demanding work.

Techniques for riding lava rock trails.
To negotiate this lava rock trail, Paul Thomasberg literally picks his way through the obstacles. Note, too, how he moves his upper body forward, backward, and from side to side to maintain bike control.

A

over the handlebars. A wheel dive with a sideways twist will lay the bike and rider down and over to the side.

If you see sand at the bottom of a descent, anticipate the problem. As you're about to hit it, shift into the low riding-the-pegs position (weight back, arms stretched forward, firm grip on the handlebars). Sitting back gets weight onto the rear wheel, so as you hit the sand, the front wheel rides freely near the surface. A firm grip keeps the front wheel straight.

There's a trick to sandy cornering. Lean into a sandy corner and both wheels will dig in and send you toppling sideways. And yet if you try to steer through a sandy corner, the front tire will dig into the sand, stick in the direction of the turn, and send you crashing. If you try to wrestle the wheel back straight, your exaggerated movements to regain control only accelerate your fall. When you come to a sandy corner, slow down, and steering ever so slightly as you go, make a wide arcing turn. Steer a bit, then straighten out the wheel, steer and straighten, and continue this routine until you've made the turn.

As summer progresses and trails get sandy or full of loose dirt, most riders I know deflate their tires. A deflated tire has more surface contact and therefore rides higher in the sand, with less resistance.

The second thing experienced sand riders do is switch tires from the

B

C

When you hit a patch of sand, sit back and lock your arms at the elbows to unweight the front wheel so that it isn't deflected off course.

narrower (1.9-inch) models to the fat (2.125- to 2.5-inch) kind. Fatter tires normally ride better in sand, and work best in it when slightly deflated.

Besting moon dust requires nothing more than a good wardrobe and a sense of impending doom. Moon-dust-riding aces wear a bandanna tied around their neck, buckeroo style. When the dust gets thick, they swing the neckerchief around to cover mouth and nose. And they steel their nerves for jolts. There always seems to be a sharp rock, huge divot, or small animal hidden under any layer of moon dust. With dust in the eyes, throat, and lungs, the moon dust rider is barely in control of his bike or his senses when Wham! he hits a hidden object and sprawls to the ground. That's why experienced mountain bikers grow to hate moon dust.

GRANITE AND RUBBLE

Granite is wonderful rock to pedal up and bike over. If you have to ride over rock, it might as well be solid granite—granite boulders, granite slabs. This rock is user friendly, certainly more so than sharp, abrasive lava or slick limestone.

However, there are times when riding over granite is demanding. Consider mountain trails covered with fine granite chips or gravel. Or those slippery little granite flakes that require a mountain biker's absolute attention. A friend calls downhill granite gravel trail riding "tiptoeing," and he's absolutely right: It's as if you're sneaking down the trail, trying desperately not to make a false move.

The best way to ride down a granite gravel trail is to slow your speed, coast along (up out of the saddle, riding the pegs), and maintain the straightest line possible. A steady pace, with your weight distributed evenly over the bike, and holding as straight a line as possible will get you through in style.

Climbing up a granite gravel trail demands staying in the saddle and never applying too much power to the rear wheel. Too much power to the pedals will cause a spinout, and standing up usually results in exactly the same thing.

Meanwhile, riding over a rock garden—a rubble-strewn section of trail—is always challenging. If the rubble just happens to be unavoidable and is on a slight downhill, don't try to pick your way through it. Get some speed up and then coast, riding the pegs, and try to maintain a straight line. Relax your upper body and arms so that they absorb shock. Pedal only if your speed drops too low.

Crossing a rubble field on the flats requires the same technique if the distance across it is short and you can gain speed before entering the field. If, however, it's a big field, add in the lift-and-lunge where necessary, and pedal to maintain momentum.

The largest, scariest rock garden I ever crossed was a half-mile-long section of rounded river rock on a fairly steep downhill. Maintaining balance, speed, and a perfect line was essential. It was like riding over greased marbles.

Like lava rock, granite requires precise riding.

HARD ROCK

America's most continuous hard-rock riding is on the Slickrock Trail outside Moab, Utah. If you've never ridden anything but dirt, sand, and rocky rubble, a trip to Slickrock is a must—the riding experience is so unique and so enjoyable. You get such incredible purchase with your tires on the rock that you feel invincible. Steep climbs, subtle moves, direction changes at slow speeds, all seem easier.

The key to slickrock riding such as you'll find at Moab is to try different techniques and see what works best. Of all the riding I've done, I think slickrock riding requires more touch, subtlety, and deftness than any other. You can't bully your bike; you have to nudge it here, steer it slightly there, lean it just a bit, balance it for a moment, pedal it hard, then slowly, then coast. It's nuance riding at its best.

Be aware that between the firm sections on a slickrock trail, there may be sandy sections. When you hit them, get into a low gear, spin through, and keep the front wheel as straight as possible.

There's nothing like slickrock to hone your technique to a fine edge.

ADOBE/CLAY

It's a tacky soil story. Two of us headed out to the Alvord Desert in southeastern Oregon. We'd ridden there before and anticipated a week of hardpack riding. We hadn't counted on 3 inches of rain and the hardpack turning into adhesive muck.

The bikes became so caked with clay that the wheels wouldn't rotate and the brakes jammed. Fortunately the sun came out, so we laid the bikes out to bake. Once we had chipped the hard-baked clay off with rocks, we were able to ride again!

The only way to beat the adobe/clay cling-on blues is to abandon all hope of forward progress and wait out the rain. Remember, it takes but a few minutes of sunshine to transform the muck back into hardpack.

SNAKEY TRAILS

If there's a rider's Nirvana, it's sure to be laced with snakey single-track trails. Single-track trails that wind downhill through forests. Trails with tight corners and plenty of obstacles.

Riding a good snakey single-track requires constant bike movement. One moment you're like a ballet dancer making a graceful swoop through a corner; the next moment you're like a boxer sticking and jabbing through ruts, around rocks, over logs. The art of single-track riding is to keep moving, changing your body position in anticipation of the next change in terrain. If you're hell-bent on really attacking a snakey downhill single-track, the only way to do it is to ride the pegs and keep looking at least 15 feet ahead, anticipating your next move.

On flat single-track trails, stay down in the saddle, pedaling to maintain speed, but stand up and ride the pegs when you come to a corner or an obstacle. Riding the pegs is the action, or alert, position.

Single-track uphills require the same basic technique: down in the saddle for most of the ride, but up out of the saddle for obstacles.

Ultimately, single-track riding is like dancing with your bike. If you're working in harmony with your two-wheeled partner, it's a wonderful feeling.

Good balance and deft
control at low speed are
the keys to successful
single-track riding.

A

Single-track uphill obstacles.
Single-track uphill obstacles are best
negotiated with a quick, succinct lift
and lunge.

LOGGING ROADS

When I talk about logging roads I refer to those wide western U.S. back roads, Forest Service roads, Bureau of Land Management roads. And my concern is how to ride them fast.

Of course the minute you start going fast down a good logging road, all the corners seem to be off-camber, pushing you out to the edge of some hoary abyss. But hey, those moments of fright are a small price to pay for a fast ride.

Carrying speed on logging roads did not come to me easily. In my early mountain biking days I would find myself riding rather timidly, wearing my brake pads down to a nubbin with a steely grip on the brake levers. Then I started riding with former off-road motorcycle racers, and they showed me the right way.

The right way is to ride the pegs, stay loose in the arms and upper body, and repeatedly squeeze and release both brakes. It's basic downhill riding

B

C

technique, but when you are carrying so much more speed on a relatively smooth, wide, open surface, you tend to forget how to do it.

It's important to keep your head up and look well down the road, and to keep body movements (except back-and-forth arm and upper body leans to absorb shock) at a minimum. The straighter your line, the better. If an obstacle suddenly appears, don't make an exaggerated move to avoid it. Tighten up your grip, and if it's not too big, plow through or over it with an aggressive lift-and-lunge.

SNOW AND ICE

There's snow and there is snow. Which is to say, some snow is easy to ride over (packed powder, thin layer of mush, hard crust) and some is extremely difficult (deep snow, ice).

The deeper the snow, the softer the snow, the more the wheels dig down and eventually halt progress. But riding a mountain bike in packed snow, or in an inch or two of new over hardpack, can be superb. I remember a winter ride when about 2 inches of slightly wet snow covered a 6-inch base of hardpack. The traction was unbelievable—better than on the same ground in the summer.

Unfortunately most snow rides are trickier. General rules for snow riding include: (1) riding a middle gear (if it's low you'll spin out; too high, you'll dig in and stall); (2) maintaining a good firm grip on the handlebars to keep the front wheel straight; (3) anglng the bike slowly to make a turn; and (4) staying down in the saddle to maintain a low center of gravity.

Snow riding requires a good "feel" for conditions. You have to learn to adapt your technique to the variations, knowing when to pedal and when to coast.

Take riding on ice, for example. It's important to get up some speed as you approach the ice. Then when you hit it, coast and ride over it, riding the pegs. Maintain a tight grip on the handlebars to keep the front wheel straight. If you slow down, give a short quick push to the pedals (no complete revolutions, just short thrusts) for speed.

On crusty snow, get in the "pounce" position to place more weight on the handlebars, and push down on the bars so that the front wheel breaks through the crust. The weight on the handlebars will help keep the front wheel straight and make a path for the rear wheel to follow.

When studded tires were introduced, they were supposed to revolutionize winter riding. They work fine, but are they worth their high cost? Experienced riders have found that by simply reducing the air pressure in their regular knobby tires, they get more contact with the snow and traction almost equal to that with studded tires.

The snow report ends with a warning: If you ride trails covered with a few inches of snow, beware of sudden surprises. The way may look smooth, but under that pristine layer of white stuff, the rocks are still round or jagged and are ready to knock you off-kilter. Take care and be prepared.

MORE OBSTACLE HOPS

Depressions

Traversing small rock-filled depressions at a slow speed can be a real problem. You can hop over most of these easily when you're going fast, but when you're going slow, you have to get out of the saddle, ride the pegs, and either lift the front wheel over or drive it through the depression. Driving the wheel through provides greater stability at lower speeds, and lifting is best at moderate speeds.

Be sure to make a couple of quick cranks on the pedals, then coast, and then lift or drive the wheel. Anticipate the shock of a wheel drive by compressing your arms downward. Bent arms absorb shock more easily.

Ditches

Broad ditches pose another problem. As you approach the edge of the ditch, you should be up in the saddle, riding the pegs, and braking to a slow roll. Roll slowly over the ditch lip, and as you do so, push your body weight onto the handlebars and release the brakes. This upper body push will drive the bike forward, down the ditch slope.

Normally you'll be carrying enough speed through the bottom of the ditch to take you up the opposite side. The key to ascending that other side is anticipation and, still on the pegs, rocking your body back quickly to pull your weight off the front wheel.

As you crest the opposite side of the ditch, rock your weight forward again, onto the handlebars, to jet the bike forward and bring the rear wheel over the top.

A   B

Ditches.

To negotiate a ditch, roll over the lip of it with your front wheel and push downward on the bike as you begin the traverse (A). Then, just as you start up the other side of the ditch, rock your body back to establish good traction on the rear wheel and to unweight the front wheel so that it doesn't plow into the ditch wall (B, C).

Rolls

The next obstacles, and perhaps the most fun, are rolls. Somewhere, someday, you'll find yourself riding over lovely roller-coaster-like bumps. One of my favorite roll rides was created when the U.S. Forest Service decided to block travel on a logging road. Boulders were bulldozed across the roadhead, and then the big Cats bladed in a quarter-mile of evenly spaced 5-foot-high dirt mounds. Thus was created one great mountain bike Coney Island.

You ride these rolls the same way you ride a broad ditch, only here you carry more speed. Gain speed as you approach the back (far) side of a roll, coast over the top, riding the pegs, then drive your upper body weight onto the handlebars for momentum down the roll, and lean and pull back as you start up the back side of the next roll. Stay loose on the pegs, working your body back and forth to keep momentum flowing forward.

Most rolls aren't that evenly spaced, so you have to pedal through the depression between them. Pedal hard enough to allow you to coast and carry momentum up and over each roll.

A

B

C

C

Topping a roll.
When topping a roll, stand high on the pegs, as shown here (A), and then drive your body forward for acceleration (B, C).

As you approach a stream, be up off the saddle with your arms locked at the elbows, so that your body is well braced when the front wheel hits the water.

Water Hazards

The last set of obstacles we have to overcome are related to water: creeks, post-rainstorm runoff ditches, and water bars.

Streams and Creeks. As a general rule, you can ride through most streams—depending on the type of rocks and bottom soil—that have up to 8 inches of water flowing through them. The deeper the water, the harder the ford.

A

Fording a stream.
Fording most shallow streams is simple if you maintain good balance, keep pedaling, and angle your bike slightly downstream.

I was not an experienced creek crosser when I got my baptism of moisture in a race that included twelve crossings. By the fifth I was getting the hang of it. However, I never mastered the 3-foot-deep stream we traversed four times. No one else did, either, but the spectators loved watching us flounder.

Let's say the streambed is firm, not too sandy, and the rocks in it are small, shot-put size, and relatively free of moss. You are on a trail approaching this stream. It looks shallow enough to be passable. The first thing to do is to make sure you're in a low gear (once in the water, shifting can throw you off balance), that the path leading to the water is obstacle-free, and that you can get up some speed.

Pedal to gain speed, and as you are about to hit the water, get up on the pegs in the "pounce" position, lock your elbows to brace your arms, and prepare for the shock of hitting the first rocks. Immediately after the hit, get more upright out of the saddle and pedal. Grip the handlebars firmly and try to keep them dead straight. Ride across at a slight downstream angle (the current seems to help you along).

There's not much more to say, except that one day a ride across old Beavertail Creek will go perfectly and the next day a rock will send you swimming. If you make sure you are carrying speed into the creek, maintain it, and keep a good grip on your handlebars, then it's up to the river gods to decide the rest.

B

C

Runoff Ruts. As fate would have it, many trails and back roads get criss-crossed with runoff ruts after a major storm. Ruts that cut across the trail or road can be a pain. Those that run down the middle can be downright nasty.

Nasty because once you're locked into one, getting out can seem impossible. Let's say you're riding along and you slip into a 3-inch runoff rut. Doesn't sound like much, does it?

But if you try to quickly steer your front wheel out of this depression, the wheel hits the rut wall, locks up in the direction of the turn, and starts to skid. The fight for bike control is on.

If you're successful in lifting the front wheel out, the rear wheel will often catch on the wall of the rut and skid sideways. As it slides downhill past the front wheel, the bike torques out of control.

There's really no established technique for downhill runoff-rut riding except to try to stay out of the ones that run straight along your path. And if you

Runoff ruts.
If you find yourself stuck in a runoff rut (A), look for a low spot in the rut and quickly lift and lunge your bike out of it (B, C).

A   B   C

do get stuck in one, to pick a spot where the rut's walls are shallow enough for an easy lift-and-lunge exit or where the rut makes a right-angle turn and lifting out is easy.

Equally difficult are deep truck tire impressions left after rain. Wherever there are dirt roads and a populace enamored of big four-wheel-drive pickups with "mountain man" tires, mountain bike riders will be fighting deep tire ruts during mud season and for months thereafter.

Getting out of a deep tire rut is tricky because, as with runoff ruts, it's hard to bring the wheels out cleanly. However, if you keep in the rut and maintain a steady, straight line, all should go well. If you swerve to avoid a rock or let your attention lapse for even a second, allowing the front wheel to hit the wall of the rut, the bike will ricochet off and out of control.

If you get stuck in a rut, it's best to stop, admit temporary defeat, and move your bike to level ground. At times such humility will save you a lot of bike-handling headaches.

Water Bars. Water bars eliminate runoff ruts on hiking, logging, and horseback trails. A water bar is a log or piece of wood, or several of them, placed across a trail and anchored at both ends. The idea is that runoff water reaching the bar is shunted off to the side of the trail, thereby preventing it from rutting the trail.

Use the basic lift-and-lunge technique to overcome water bars. Never ride around their ends. Riding around water bars creates a new path for water to flow down and erode the trail.

Always go over, not around, water bars.

STREET SMARTS

Every trick you learn riding off-road will help your on-road experience. The only road techniques that require more explanation are those for negotiating curbs and descending steps.

Curbs

When you want to hop over a curb, make sure your bike is at a right angle to it. If you approach the curb at an acute angle, the front wheel can deflect, sending the bike, and you, out of control.

    Turn your bike in a wide arc so that it is lined up perpendicular to the curb,

Negotiating a curb.
The easiest way to climb a curb is to perform a slow lift of the front wheel (A) and a simple forward lunge to clear the rear wheel (B, C).

coast slowly toward the curb (brake if you're carrying too much speed), lift up aggressively on the handlebars, and then lunge forward after the front wheel has gone over the curb.

Slow is good when curb-hopping. So is watching for pedestrians. Brake until you're going slowly. Slow speed minimizes the wheel impact and helps you get a good powerful lift to clear the curb.

Coming off that curb, again go slowly. Ride the pegs upright, with weight on your arms and on the handlebars. As you drop off the curb, bend your arms a bit to absorb the shock, and after the rear wheel plops down, pedal off.

If you're feeling roguish and the way is clear, get up some speed and "bunny hop" on and off curbs. It's a showy move and it eliminates the jarring rear wheel plop.

B

C

A   B

Hopping off a curb.
When hopping off a curb, ride the pegs and flex your arms (A) to absorb the shock from the impact (B).

The bunny hop.
For style points, bunny-hop the curb just as you would a wilderness obstacle.

A   B

Steps

Riding down steps is a whole other matter. You have to know when the angle of the steps is too steep and when the steps are too widely spaced. The ideal steps are close, evenly spaced, and drop at a moderate angle.

Why even bother with step riding? Mainly because it's fun, different, and as I found in Korea during the '88 Olympics, a real social icebreaker. Since most of the athletic stadiums in Seoul had stairs leading to and from their main gates, I indulged in a bit of step descending—all right, showing off. It never failed to attract a crowd, and it got me in touch with new Korean friends.

Back at the Press Village, a daily descent of the steps leading from the guardhouse to the Village grounds indelibly stamped my image into the brains of the machine-gun-toting guards. When the day came that I forgot my entry identification, they remembered my daily steps antics and, against all rules, let me pass.

Step riding isn't recommended for everyone. If you try it, do the following: ride the pegs back off the saddle; keep a firm, unwavering grip on the handlebars; go for it without braking, carrying speed; and concentrate. That's it. May your step descents be brilliant.

Yes, you can ride down steps. Just ride the pegs, back your rear off the saddle, maintain a firm grip on the handlebars, and keep your head up and your eyes forward.

PRESSURE SITUATION

This may seem to be the wrong place to talk about tire pressure, but now that we've gone over various types of terrain, it's the best time discuss this airy issue.

Basically the rule is that the lower the air pressure (20 to 30 pounds), the softer the ride and the higher the rate of tube punctures; the higher the pressure (40 to 60 pounds), the harder the ride and the lower the puncture rate.

Compromise is the best way to get a decent ride and avoid flats. I ride with 40 pounds of pressure in the front tire and 42 pounds in the rear. That makes for a fairly rough ride, but I don't find myself patching many tires.

I reduce that pressure by 10 pounds when I'm riding in deep sand or soft snow. Also, if I know a route well and it has a section of smooth road with lots of corners, I deflate my tires for a more controlled ride. At the end of the section, I pump the tires back up to the normal pressure.

Urban guerilla.
Sometimes when dealing with urban obstacles, you have to do a little guerilla riding, as Paul Thomasberg does here. Note, however, that all his riding techniques, from rounding the curve (A) to negotiating a bumpy downhill (B, C, D), are equally applicable in the wilds.

A

B

C

D

7

Trials Techniques

Years ago motorcyclists dreamed up a competition to test their bike-handling skills at slow speeds. The object was to ride a short, tight, obstacle-filled course without getting hung up on an obstacle or touching a foot down for balance.

They called the event "trials," and it became so popular that manufacturers began producing "trials bikes" with ultra-high clearance and extremely low gearing.

Taking its cue from motorcycle competitions, bicycle trials riding is an esoteric part of the mountain biking sport, and when done in competition, requires a specially designed small bike frame with a high bottom bracket, single-speed gearing, and two sturdy brakes.

We'll cover basic trials technique with the hope that if you get a chance to watch an official trials competition, you'll be knowledgeable about what you're seeing. And if you do get a chance, by all means go; the top trials riders will amaze you with their bike-handling skills.

For everyday mountain bike riding, trials technique means learning how to handle your bike at low, almost no, speed. So why learn it at all? Because the time will come when you're on a trail that demands slow speed and delicate manuevering. Either you learn to ride these tricky trails or you end up walking your bike. The fun is in riding, not walking.

When I think of trials riding, I think of a phrase used many times by U.S. kayak champion and Olympic competitor Eric Evans to describe the key kayak slalom technique. The phrase is "pause and pounce." The kayaker collects his energies, then pounces through a slalom gate, over a falls, or into an eddy. Similarly, the mountain biker pauses (coasts at low speed), then pounces (a short burst of power to the pedals, a sharp lift on the handlebars, a quick bike lean, a quick steer, complete braking).

135

Leaping off huge boulders with a single bound, the trials rider is mountain biking's superman.

On a normal-size mountain bike, trials courses get tougher.

The basic trials riding position is upright on the pegs, and the basic pedal strokes are quick quarter-revolution bursts, with a few quick full turns as you approach a log or rock along the obstacle course. Trials courses generally include unusual combinations of large obstacles, particularly big rocks and thick logs. If a trials rider is not aggressive with his lift-and-lunge, those logs and rocks can jam a bike's large chainring in an instant. The rider has to approach with a burst of speed, make an all-out lift, and then lunge forward forcefully with a couple of revolutions on the cranks to keep the momentum going.

Deftness, however, is what's needed to steer neatly around minor impediments at slow speed. Here the technique is subtle steering with quick returns of the wheel to the straight-ahead position.

The same subtlety applies in making quick leans and quick pushes on the pedals for just the right amount of oomph. Too much of either and the rider topples. The key is to pause (brake to a standstill and balance the bike for an instant), check out the next move, and then pounce (power up, then power over or glide past the obstacle).

Without having seen a mountain bike trials, you may find all of this a little abstract. And the concept of bouncing up and down on your bike as if it were a two-wheeled pogo stick before hopping up over a log must seem downright weird. But bouncing the bike is an important advanced trials riding technique. Good bounce technique requires steady balance on the bike when it's not moving and precise timing to lift it high off the ground and move it either in a new direction (180 degrees is typical) or up onto a rock or log. To aid balance and bounce, trials riders keep their tire pressure low.

Let's look at an example: A trials competition course has a huge rock in it. To "clean" this section of the course (not lose any points), the competitors have to get their bikes up onto the top of the rock without touching a foot to the ground.

As a rider approaches the rock, he slows and brakes the bike to a complete stop. Standing on the pegs, he vigorously bounces the bike up and down, and then, with a dynamic upward pull of arms and legs, lifts the bike up into the air and uses his upper body to direct the bike toward the top of the rock. If the landing is successful, the rider will immediately start to bounce the bike to maintain balance, and then slowly hop it to the rock's edge for a quick hop back to the ground.

Trials *are* weird—and wonderful to watch. They aren't for everyone, but let's face it, knowing a few basic trials techniques can only enhance your backcountry riding skills.

B A

Using the bounce technique, trials riders often confront obstacles typically avoided by other mountain bikers.

As ace trials rider Jim Terhaar demonstrates, trials riding is not without its dangers. In attempting to hop off a high rock, Jim catches his rear wheel and—well—ends up wishing he hadn't. (For a look at the consequence of this fall, see page 145.)

A B C

D

E

8

Ecology, Etiquette, and Safety

Every year there are reports of mountain bikes and bikers being banned from trails because of the damage they've caused or because of nasty encounters with other people on the trails. Both situations are avoidable. It is important to respect the trails, the ecology around the trails, and the rights of other trail users.

ECOLOGY

Skids and Skidding. Skidding around corners may seem like a macho thing to do, but it's very uncool. The skid marks of summer become the rainy season's eroded ruts. Bring your bike's speed down slowly by pumping the brakes, and glide around corners. And never purposefully skid to a stop.

Water Bars. Water bars are embedded in trails to prevent erosion. Don't go around the water bar's ends. If you do, the tire marks become a path down which water can flow and begin eroding the trail once more.

Wilderness. Wilderness areas are set aside to provide people with a pristine natural experience. Mountain bikes are restricted from wilderness areas, although it's debatable as to why when, in most cases, horses are allowed to trample them. But as long as mountain bikes are prohibited, mountain bikers should honor that restriction.

Fragile Ground. Tundra, wet clay soils, and marshland all should be avoided if possible. One tire track across such delicate soil can mar it for years. Don't be a slob rider who has to put his or her personal tire print on every square inch of backcountry. Avoid fragile ground when you ride.

Basic trail etiquette and an awareness of others' rights and needs help ease trail-use conflicts.

Forget skidding your wheels: it's not considered cool and it can harm trails and ecosystems.

Stay out of posted areas—respect both wilderness and private property.

Animal Habitats. If the sign says "Restricted—Animal Habitat," obey it. A mountain bike gives you access to remote areas, but that doesn't give you the right to invade every creature's privacy.

TRAIL ETIQUETTE

We live in a time when etiquette is all but dead, but that doesn't exempt mountain bikers from their responsibility to be courteous to fellow trail users. If you know a bike trail is shared with horseback riders and hikers, yield them the right of way.

It's imperative to stop and dismount as soon as you see a horse approaching. Lay your bike down and stand between it and the horse. Make sure you're on a level lower than the horse while you do this; equestrians tell me that if a person stands above a horse on a trail, the horse thinks it's about to be

IMBA Rules of the Trail

1. Ride on open trails only. Respect trail and road closures (ask if not sure); avoid possible trespass on private land; obtain permits and authorization as may be required. Federal and State wilderness areas are closed to cycling.

2. Leave no trace. Be sensitive to the dirt beneath you. Even on open trails, you should not ride under conditions where you will leave evidence of your passing, such as on certain soils shortly after a rain. Observe the different types of soils and trail construction; practice low-impact cycling. This also means staying on the trail and not creating any new ones. Be sure to pack out at least as much as you pack in.

3. Control your bicycle! Inattention for even a second can cause disaster. Excessive speed maims and threatens people; there is no excuse for it!

4. Always yield the trail. Make known your approach well in advance. A friendly greeting (or a bell) is considerate and works well; startling someone may cause loss of trail access. Show your respect when passing others by slowing to a walk or even stopping. Anticipate that other trail users may be around corners or in blind spots.

5. Never spook animals. All animals are startled by an unannounced approach, a sudden movement, or a loud noise. This can be dangerous for you, for others, and for the animals. Give animals extra room and time to adjust to you. In passing, use special care and follow the directions of horseback riders (ask if uncertain). Running cattle and disturbing wild animals is a serious offense. Leave gates as you found them, or as marked.

6. Plan ahead. Know your equipment, your ability, and the area in which you are riding—and prepare accordingly. Be self-sufficient at all times. Wear a helmet, keep your machine in good condition, and carry necessary supplies for changes in weather or other conditions. A well-executed trip is a satisfaction to you and not a burden or offense to others.

Reprinted courtesy of International Mountain Bicycling Association (IMBA), Route 2, Box 303, Bishop, CA 93514.

pounced on. Allow the horseback rider to calm his mount and ride past before you climb back on your own mount.

Slow down for hikers and give them an opportunity to step off the trail before you pass by—or stop, step off the bike, and let them pass. And when you pass by, be sure to say "thank you." A little good will goes a long way and helps ease trail user conflicts.

Public Works. If the opportunity arises to work with the Forest Service, Bureau of Land Management, or state, local, or regional park people on trail maintenance, do so. Get a volunteer group together and pitch in. Donating time and labor will pay dividends when new trails are opened and the question comes up as to whether or not mountain bikers should be allowed to use them.

GENERAL SAFETY CONSIDERATIONS

On any trail, maintain controlled speed on downhills. Controlling your speed means you'll have a safe trip and will be able to avert collisions with other riders or with animals and nonmoving obstacles, such as downed trees.

Low speed is mandatory on a first ride down a new trail. You have no idea where the blind corners, ruts, fallen trees, and sheer drop-offs are. Take it slow. Learn the trail's ways before increasing your speed.

Another important safety concern is making sure everything is in order in your repair kit—especially the spare tube and patch materials—before you take off on a backcountry ride.

If the weather looks as if it might drizzle or rain, make sure you take along a rain jacket. To be doubly safe, take along a synthetic underwear top. That will give you an added layer of insulative warmth should you get too chilly.

Other safety essentials include good eyewear, to protect your eyes from flying stones, low-hanging branches, and bugs; good protective padded gloves, to reduce the effect of road shock on your hands and arms and to protect your hands in case of a fall; and of course a decent helmet, to protect that fragile head.

Bruises, Scrapes, and Breaks

The most common trail injuries are bruises and scrapes: a rider goes down on his side and scrapes a lot of skin off his leg, or hits a branch with his shoulder, a rock with his leg, and bruises both. Bruises are something you have to live with for the rest of the ride. Scrapes and cuts, on the other hand, should be cleaned before you continue on your way. Your backcountry first-aid kit should contain some sterile gauze pads, a small tube of liquid soap, Bacitracin ointment, a small roll of adhesive tape, and a clean bandanna.

For scrapes, use the bandanna and some water from your water bottle to get most of the dirt off; then using a sterile gauze pad, scrub with soap and

It took nine stitches to close this gash. First aid included staunching the flow of blood with a sterile gauze pad and irrigating the wound gently with soap and water. See page 138 for how it happened.

water; and let the area dry. Add a light coating of Bacitracin and leave the scrape exposed or cover with a pad, depending on the severity. (Caution: Unless you're in the high mountains where the streams run crystal clear, cleaning a wound with stream or river water can cause infection.)

On cuts, stop the bleeding with pressure to the wound. Clean it carefully with soap and water, using a sterile gauze pad, and then cover with a pad. Do not use an antiseptic on the cut as it will inhibit healing.

Remember: Clean wounds heal, dirty ones get infected. Last fall I went for a long ride the day before leaving on a European tour, on which I planned to indulge in fattening foods and great wine. During the ride I crashed and scraped my knee badly. I thought I'd cleaned the wounds thoroughly on the trail, and again later at home. Wrong. I was barely through my first day in Europe when my knee puffed up to the size of a softball. I spent the first week of vacation hobbling around and gulping antibiotics every four hours.

For cuts that require stitches, you and those with you have to decide how bad the cut is. If it's a deep gash that's bleeding profusely, then the injured person should be immobilized and one fellow rider should try to staunch the bleeding while another heads out for help.

The other situation in which a rider has to go for help is when someone breaks a bone. In my years of riding, I've encountered two instances, both in races, when a rider broke a collarbone in a fall over the handlebars. For any break, immobilize the rider and seek help.

Detailed first-aid instruction is beyond the scope of this book. For more on general medical safety, I suggest consulting Dr. Paul S. Auerbach's *Medicine for the Outdoors* (Little, Brown and Company, 1986).

Hot-Weather Riding

On hot days rest when you start to overheat, drink plenty of fluids, and cool off with stream water if you can.

Exhaustion

It's a hot summer day and you're climbing a long exposed hill. You start to get dizzy, a bit disoriented, and your head starts to pound. If this ever happens to you, watch out: you're overheating and heading toward heat exhaustion—which can lead to heat stroke, convulsions, coma, and even death.

Simply put, heat exhaustion starts when the body absorbs too much heat and cannot dissipate it. Normally, body temperature is regulated by perspiration, which cools the skin as it evaporates. However, there are days when we literally "boil over."

When you feel heat exhaustion coming on, get out of the sun and into the shade. Rest, and drink as much fluid as possible. The veteran rider will avoid riding on the hot days, but if he has to, he will take along at least two extra-large water bottles.

If you have to ride when it's hot, go at a slow pace, drink regularly, and at the first sign of dizziness, get out of the sun. If you feel faint and a stream or lake is close by, peel your clothes off and lie in the water for 15 minutes to lower your body temperature.

In 1978 I ran a 10-kilometer mountain running race in extreme heat (103 degrees). I overheated badly and was pretty delirious when I finished the race. After an hour of rest under a shade tree, with someone pouring water over my head and neck at regular intervals, I was back to normal.

My running partner fared far worse. After crossing the finish line, he collapsed and went into convulsions. A quick-acting medical team carried him to a glacial lake 50 yards away and immersed him in the water for an hour. The cool water brought his body temperature down and saved his life.

Later, in the now long departed and lamented Whiskeytown Downhill mountain bike race outside Redding, California, the temperature at the race start (7:00 A.M.) was 100 degrees. As the long (3-to-4-hour) race progressed, it got unbearably hot. Fortunately the race course crossed several cold mountain streams—and each one was packed with bodies cooling down as the race and the racers heated up.

A good rule of the trail is to drink plenty of liquids before a ride on a hot day, and to keep on drinking them as the ride goes along. Also, when things get hot, pour some water from your water bottle over your neck, or soak a bandanna in water and tie it around your neck to keep something cool against your skin.

Hypothermia

Hypothermia is deadly, and contrary to the common lore that it occurs only on cold wintry days, most hypothermia deaths occur on cool damp days or, especially in the mountains, on days that start hot and dry but turn cold and rainy. In both instances, people can die if they don't have the proper clothing to protect them from the elements.

A typical mountain biking hypothermia scenario might go like this: A group heads out on a warm spring day for a mountain trail ride. They expect to be out for a couple of hours, so they are traveling light. An hour into the ride, someone breaks a chain, and after repairing it, the group experiences further delays getting around new-fallen timber across the trail. Then the group takes a wrong turn. The short ride has become a half-day epic.

To make up for lost time, the riders go hard. Everyone is sweat-soaked when, an hour from home, a cold rainstorm hits. Soon the riders are soaked to the bone. They ride on, the wind chilling their bodies literally to the core. Soon they begin to shake uncontrollably; someone inexplicably rides off the trail; the simple act of shifting seems impossible. Hypothermia has set in.

Hypothermia occurs when the body is chilled well below its normal temperature. If not treated immediately, it can sap a victim's energy resources within hours, killing him.

There is mild hypothermia and profound hypothermia. Mild hypothermia is typified by a sudden lack of interest in your well-being (except for getting warm), shaking (the body trying to warm itself up), loss of muscle control, and, later on, disorientation.

Profound hypothermia—when the body core temperature drops below 90 degrees)—is typified by altered mental functioning. The victim exhibits abnormal behavior and simultaneously loses muscle function. Suddenly he or she doesn't seem to care about getting warm anymore.

Mild hypothermia is easily treated by donning dry, warm, protective clothes, drinking something warm, and getting into a warm environment. It can be avoided on a mountain bike trip by being prepared (hypothermia is often called the "killer of the unprepared").

Never make a mountain ride without carrying rain gear, an extra shirt (or a synthetic long underwear top), and a few candy bars. At the first sign of rain or changing weather, put on the rain gear on to keep your body from getting wet and wind-chilled. If the weather gets colder, add the underwear layer next to your skin. It will trap rising body heat and form an insulative barrier against the cold.

If you start to shake a bit, eat the candy bars. They will give your blood sugar a jolt and help keep you warm. If things get really bad, stop riding, get under a tree's canopy and huddle together with the other riders to conserve heat.

Profound hypothermia is a different story. The mortality rate varies from

50 to 80 percent. The victim has to be rewarmed slowly (too fast and he might suffer rewarming shock). If someone gets profoundly hypothermic on a ride, the others riders must do all they can (huddling around him, getting dry clothes on him) to stabilize the condition until he can be evacuated to a hospital. A hypothermia victim can remain in a stable cold state for a long time without danger to his life.

For more good information on hypothermia, I recommend Wilkerson, Bangs, and Hayward's *Hypothermia, Frostbite and Other Cold Injuries* (Seattle: The Mountaineers, 1986.)

Having been mildly hypothermic several times, I have my personal prevention secret: along with a rain jacket and spare underwear top, I carry a tightly knit wool watch cap on backcountry trips and put it on under my helmet when things get cold and rainy. Since at least 50 percent of one's body heat can escape through the head, my wool watch cap helps keep hypothermia at bay.

Altitude Sickness

Most people think of altitude sickness as something that happens only to mountaineers on a high-altitude climb. Surprisingly, there are more reported (and unreported) cases of acute mountain sickness—the basic form of altitude sickness—at low elevations (6,000 to 9,000 feet) than there are at higher elevations. More typical than the mountaineer having altitude sickness problems is the flatland vacationer experiencing it during his first day on the tennis court or ski slope at a Colorado mountain resort.

The primary cause of acute mountain sickness is a low percentage of oxygen in the blood flowing to the brain. Blood vessels in the brain dilate when blood oxygen saturation is decreased, and the dilation causes headaches. Other symptoms include dizziness, fatigue, shortness of breath, nausea, vomiting, and a range of flu-like symptoms.

If you're riding up a long mountain trail and you feel dizzy or nauseated, it's time to stop and rest. When you feel better, turn your bike downhill and head for lower terrain. Usually it takes only a slight drop in elevation to relieve the symptoms and make you start to feel better.

Sometimes, just riding along a flat road or trail on your first day in higher elevations makes you ill. If this happens, take a day off and rest in order to acclimatize yourself—rest usually does the job. If it doesn't, though, see a doctor, who might prescribe a drug such as Diamox to relieve the problem.

For more insight on acute mountain sickness and other high-altitude problems, read *Medicine for Mountaineering* (Seattle: The Mountaineers, 1985), edited by James A. Wilkerson, M.D.

9

Fat-Tire Touring

No matter what you call it—touring, saddlebagging, bike backpacking—using a mountain bike for back-road/backcountry camping trips and extended road tours makes sense. Add a few of the right accessories, and your mountain bike becomes a rugged, stable touring machine.

For any tour, off- or on-road, racks and panniers are a must: racks to hold a tent, sleeping bag, and sleeping pad, and the panniers for clothing, food, and cooking items. Front and rear racks are attached to the frame by inserting screws into eyelets. For example, a rear rack is anchored in two places: on the bike's rear triangle, near its junction with the top and seat tubes of the main triangle; and at the end of the chainstays, by means of legs that extend down from the rack. Your bike must have the proper eyelets for rack attachment.

Racks attached, it's time to consider panniers. "Pannier" comes from the Latin *panarium,* meaning breadbasket, and over the years has come to mean cyclists' saddlebags. Panniers lie over the top of a rear or front rack the same way a saddlebag lies over the back of a horse or a mule. Bicycle panniers are attached to the rack by straps or clips. There are not that many different pannier designs. What distinguishes one model from another is generally the storage capacity, which is measured in cubic inches.

Storage capacity is a tricky issue in touring. You may opt for the most voluminous panniers available, only to find that once filled they have an adverse effect on bike handling. The heavy load shifts, the bike sways, and control becomes a problem. On the other hand, if you get smaller-capacity panniers, they may not hold enough for an extended trip. If possible, get in touch with an active mountain bike tourer and get his or her ideas on pannier capacity. Try to ride that person's bike when it's loaded for a tour.

On- or off-road, panniers do affect bike handling. Before heading out on

151

With map in hand and everything but the kitchen sink in panniers, a mountain bike tourer charts his course.

Panniers.
A typical pair of front-load panniers, with a sleeping bag stuff sack strapped on top of the rack.

Rear racks with side panniers and a top pack. Note the spare tire—a necessity on any tour—nested between the seat post and the rack.

any tour, make a few practice rides to see how a load affects your bike. Also, don't undertake a nasty, gnarly, backcountry single-track tour when fully loaded unless you're into torture. The best backcountry tours are on done with manageable loads on logging roads or moderately difficult trails.

After racks and panniers, the next most important purchase is camping gear. Don't skimp here. Cheap, leaky tents and thin, uninsulative sleeping bags have brought many a tour to a close after one uncomfortable night. Of all the camping essentials, a good tent is the most important. There are dozens of small, compact models made for cycle touring. These lightweight tents are generally snug solo or cramped two-person designs. They do work, but I view them more as emergency shelters than as tents. Personally, I feel that the added weight of a larger, freestanding mountaineering tent, which allows you more freedom of movement, is minute compared to the pleasure of camping in a tent like this.

A larger two-person tent gives you a palace to live in when you're traveling solo (a plus when you're in for a couple of days of lousy weather) and a comfortable, uncramped abode for two when you're traveling with a companion. (When traveling with a partner, let one person carry the rain fly and poles and the other the tent's main body; this cuts the weight per cyclist to a minimum.)

Important criteria to look for in a superior tent are that it is freestanding (stands by itself without guy lines) and that it comes with shock-corded aluminum poles (the cord allows poles to be extended and broken down without fitting or unfitting each pole section), a rain fly (keeps the rain off the main body of the tent), and mosquito-netting doors and windows (to keep the bugs at bay). When considering a tent, look to mountaineering and backpacking gear manufacturers—names like Sierra Designs, The North Face, Kelty, Gregory, Eureka, and REI (Recreational Equipment Incorporated).

The same quest for quality applies to sleeping bags, with the mountaineering/backpacking companies making the best. In purchasing a bag, there are two types to consider: down and synthetic. Genuine goose-down bags are more expensive but offer an unrivaled high-warmth-to-light-weight ratio. They can be stuffed small for easy rack storage. Their drawback: if the down gets wet, it clumps and loses its insulative loft. Synthetic bags, on the other hand, will

A roomy two-person freestanding tent is a mansion for the solo tourer.

keep you warm if they get wet and require less care, but they are bulkier and heavier. There has been a lot of innovation in synthetic fills during the past few years, and as a result synthetic sleeping bags are becoming less bulky. They are also becoming more expensive, but are still reasonably priced in comparison to down bags.

Which sleeping bag you buy comes down to getting what best meets your camping needs within your price range. If weight, warmth, and compactness are important, then buy a down bag with a waterproof stuff sack. If price, low upkeep, and warmth even if the bag gets wet are important, then a synthetic bag is best. Whichever type of bag you choose, be sure to pair it with a good sleeping pad. After years of sleeping on an ensolite foam pad, I decided that a bit more weight on the bike was worth the comfort of a self-inflating air mattress. Suddenly I had no more sleepless nights, no more stiffness come morning.

Among non-camping items to consider are security locks, tires, and spare parts. The next chapter covers locks in detail, but suffice it to say here that security is particularly important on any road tour.

And if you are touring strictly on paved roads, it's best to remove your knobby tires and put on bald slicks (slicks are also discussed in detail in the next chapter). These tires create less rolling resistance because of their smooth-ness and because they can be inflated much firmer than a knobby tire.

No matter what kind of tour you take—on- or off-road—always take along a spare tire. And to your repair kit (see Chapter 11) add extra spokes, brake cable, gear cable, and a spare rear derailleur.

PACKING IT UP

Once you have all your touring gear together, practice packing it up, and take several test rides on your loaded bike. Put soft clothing items at the bottom of each pannier compartment and heavier, clunkier stuff close to the bike frame (to keep the bike from leaning excessively to either side). Try to balance the load equally on both sides of the bike, and if you're using two sets of panniers, over the front and rear wheels.

Store your tent on one rack, your sleeping bag on the other. Wrap the tent in your sleeping pad.

When you practice packing, be sure to include food, stove, stove fuel, and kitchen utensils (if you plan to cook), as well as snacks for the road. Top off the load with emergency clothing (rain gear, sweater). Then take your loaded bike out for a ride to get used to the way it handles.

A heavy, but perfectly balanced, load.

If you're planning a backcountry tour, practice riding off-road. Make sure you ride up a long hill while standing out of the saddle. This will give you a good indication of how the bike's normal side-to-side tipping is affected by the added weight.

Next, try to ride a shorter, steeper hill while seated. If the front end bucks up excessively, you may want to add more weight to the front panniers.

If the rear end slides excessively when you brake on a short, steep downhill, you might have to shift even more weight to the rear panniers.

If you're planning a road tour, go out for a short ride to get a feel for weight distribution and overall changes in bike handling. Steering will be slower, and you'll have to anticipate sooner in order to negotiate obstacles or, if necessary, bring the bike to a complete stop.

RIDING WITH THE PACK

Many off-road backcountry tourers don't like, and don't use, panniers. They feel that they interfere with bike handling and reduce the joy of backcountry riding.

I agree, and for short trips I prefer to use an internal-frame rucksack to carry clothing, food, and sleeping bag while storing my tent and sleeping pad on a rear rack.

A good bike-packing rucksack is one of what is known as a day-and-a-half

This tourer is off for a weekend of fly fishing, with all his gear contained in one rucksack.

Another way to carry your fly rod: rig a length of PVC tubing to your bike and you're on your way! The scene is the Deschutes River in central Oregon.

design. These packs are slim, medium-capacity models. They have a wide hip belt with a quick-release plastic buckle system and a buckle-operated sternum strap across the chest.

Cinch the hip belt and sternum strap down, and your load is held close to the body. As your body moves, the load moves with you. (Contrast this with the pannier-loaded bike, where when the bike moves, you react to go with or to inhibit that movement.)

Obviously rucksack touring isn't desirable for long road tours (although I did one in England and it wasn't *that* bad), but for gnarly backcountry trail riding I believe it's the better way to go. Better because bike handling is easier and because you tend to pack smarter, taking just what you need, not what you think you might need.

Give the rucksack method a try on short tours. It can save you pannier purchase money—money that could be used toward the purchase of a better tent.

If you want tips on setting up camp and avoiding the usual camping hazards, I refer you to *Sports Illustrated Backpacking* by Jack McDowell (New York: Sports Illustrated Winner's Circle Books, 1989). And remember, the movement in camping these days is toward the low-impact variety. That means not only packing out what you pack in, but endeavoring to leave no trace whatever of your stay.

RULES OF THE ROAD

Whenever you use your mountain bike for a road tour, be prepared by learning the bicycle rules of the road for each state you'll pass through. State laws regarding bicycle use will vary, and it's good to know ahead of time what to expect.

If you're riding on well-traveled roads, begin your riding an hour after sunrise and end it an hour before sunset. It's difficult for drivers to see cyclists at dawn and at dusk, so there's greater risk riding during those low-light times.

For added safety, wear brightly colored clothes on bright days and a reflective sash or vest on overcast days. The idea is to let motorists know you're on the road. Blending in with the scenery is courting disaster.

Many bike touring companies equip their rental bikes with an aerial-like wand with a bright neon-colored flag at its tip. The waving flag is supposed to warn approaching vehicles that someone/something is on the road ahead. The idea is sound, but I've found that bright clothing does the job just as well, or better.

On the road, always keep a straight, steady line. Don't weave from side to side or waver suddenly out into the highway. If you have to make a quick move to avoid an obstacle (and there are loads of these along any well-traveled road), weave *away* from the traffic if you can, or stop completely and either move the obstacle or lift your bike over it.

If you have to stop for a breather, drink of water, snack, repair, or whatever, pull well off the road. Don't trust to luck when you are resting on the edge of the roadway, and never make a repair there. Get off the road for safety's sake.

Never listen to a portable tape deck or radio—especially the kind with earphones—while riding. You *must* be able to hear approaching traffic so you can be prepared to move out of the way if necessary.

Finally, always ride defensively and be ready to pull off the road in a flash should you encounter a problem. This is very important on narrow country and mountain roads, where traffic can get too close for comfort.

Fit your bike with a pair of slick tires and a rear rack, and it's off to work you go.

10

City Slicker

The mountain bike is the perfect commuter vehicle, provided that you don't need to pedal on the interstate and that you change tires, add a rear rack, and consider adding fenders during the rainy season.

SLICKS

The tire change should be from knobbies to slicks, a catchall term used to describe bald, smooth, fat rubber tires that roll along the road with less resistance. Ride your bike around town one morning with knobbies; then replace them with slicks and repeat your morning ride. You'll be amazed. Slicked up, on paved streets you'll feel as if you're flying.

For all their good qualities, slicks do look a bit weird. I have slicks on my town bike—the Purple People Eater—and I'm constantly quizzed as to how they ride, whether or not they go flat too easily, how well they handle on wet pavement, and so on.

After four years of heavy slick city riding, I've had zero flats. My wife has had one flat in the same period of time, and hers came from an industrial staple lodged in Montana blacktop. Flats are no more a problem than with any other tire, although I admit I watch the roads carefully for sharp debris.

I scoffed when slicks were first introduced. How could they possibly be good on wet streets? Well, Avocet, a company that makes fat slicks (as does Specialized Bicycle Components), ran an advertisement showing a rider cornering sharply with slick tires on wet pavement. I decided to test their advertised claim, and have yet to slide out of control cornering on slick streets.

Slicks can be inflated to higher pressures (100 psi is typical) which, along

Mountain bike slicks are fat, bald, and lovable.

with their smooth surface, reduces road resistance. They can also be run at low pressure in sand and over rock.

One dry summer, every trail near home turned to sand. Knobby tires, no matter how deflated, just weren't getting the traction, so a group of us tested slicks on the sand. We ran them at about 35 psi and found that they could grip and pass through the deep sand with ease.

Later, while on a week-long road tour through Montana, a friend and I decided to climb a rocky trail that led to the summit of a 10,000-foot peak. The ride was a slow one over long granite slabs and through patches of granitic rubble and gravel. I reduced the pressure in my slicks and discovered that they gripped the rock like the rubber on a good technical climbing shoe. On the other hand, my friend had problems with his knobby tires' hard rubber lugs not gripping and, as a result, spinning frustratingly on the rock.

Another time, I rode Utah's Slickrock trail with knobbies and then with slicks. The winner? Well, I got better grip and better control with slicks.

So while I might not use slicks for everyday trail riding, I do find that they are versatile tires, perfect for commuting around town and also excellent for specialized off-road use.

REAR RACKS

Back to city streets, where the next best addition to your fat-tire commuter flyer is a rear rack. Nothing holds a briefcase, lunch box, or workout clothes bag better. A couple of quality bungee cords should keep any modest-size load securely attached to the rack, and for drizzly days, you can add a snap-on plastic rack cover to keep water off your backside. These covers work well, but they won't keep items on the rack perfectly dry. When it's drizzly, carry your work papers, spare clothes, and so on in a waterproof daypack or rucksack.

FENDERS

Now, if you're a truly dedicated bike commuter, you'll want to add fenders during the rainy season. There are several different types available, all designed to keep front wheel spray off your face and rear wheel spray off your navy blue blazer. Fenders are lightweight, easy to install, and worth it—especially when it pours.

LOCKING DEVICES

When you get to work on a rainy day, ideally you'll be able to store your bike indoors. If not, be sure to remove the saddle and take it inside. For that matter, as a general rule it's always a good idea to take the saddle and the front wheel off your bike when you lock it outside in an urban area. Never just lock the frame to a lamppost, fence, or railing. Make sure you secure the frame and rear wheel, and take the seat and front wheel with you. I've seen bikes firmly locked to a permanant fixture in the morning, only to be stripped of both wheels and seat by early afternoon. Therefore, besides taking the seat and front wheel with you, double-lock your bike. Use one of the heavy U-shaped, virtually indestructible locks (Gorilla and Kryptonite are two brands) to lock the frame to the post, fence, or railing, and a cable lock to secure the rear wheel to both the frame and the anchor point.

The U-shaped locks are key locks; cables can be used with either a combination lock or a key lock. For optimum security, always use a stout key lock. Bike thieves can knock off a combination lock in seconds.

Now, raise your right hand and repeat the following bike commuter's security credo out loud:

Lock-up

No bike lock-up method is foolproof, but here's a pretty good one that utilizes a cable around the wheels connected to a U-clamp around both the seat post and a convenient street post.

Perhaps a better method: lock the front and rear wheels together with a U-clamp.

You might also want to lock your bike's seat to the wheels or the frame.

I will use two locks to secure my bike;

I will secure the frame with one lock and the rear wheel with another;

I will remove the front wheel and saddle and take them with me wherever I go;

If I work for an enlightened employer, I will make sure he provides secure inside storage for bicycles;

And I will always wear a helmet for personal security.

RULES OF THE ROAD II

In the preceding chapter we covered the rules of the road for open road touring. Many of the same rules apply for urban riding, including the one about knowing state and local cycling laws.

For city riding, you have to adapt a thoroughly defensive attitute. Ride as though trouble lurks at every corner, and anticipate what you'll do to avoid it. You have to be ever-aware that pedestrians will suddenly step off the curb out in front of you, that cars will abruptly make a turn in front of you, cutting you off, that side-view mirrors can sideswipe you, that a parked car's driver's-side door will open suddenly into the street, blocking your way.

Stay alert, with your head up and your eyes focused and darting, looking at the traffic ahead and to your side. Never try that Tour de France head-down sprint in city traffic.

Use the same arm turn signals outlined in the state's driver's manual. Normally that's the left arm extended straight out to indicate a left turn, and bent upward at the elbow, forming a 90-degree angle, to indicate a right turn. And for heaven's sake, be vocal and animated! Make the proper arm signal, and then follow it up with a series of vigorous finger points and arm jabs in the direction you're planning to turn. Yell at drivers if they have their windows open: let them know you're there and are turning. Put a little drama, a little stagecraft, into your turns—it will help people notice and avoid you.

If you ride in a big, big city (New York, Los Angeles, Chicago), either carry a whistle or have a loud bell or horn mounted on your handlebars. Use the whistle, bell, or horn to let pedestrians and cars know you're there. (Come to think of it, any of these noisemakers can be handy in a small city, too.)

Most human obstacles respond to sound. Those other obstacles—potholes, drainage grates—don't. I remember a fairly hair-raising ride through the streets

When riding in urban settings, stay alert to what's going on around you.

of lower Manhattan that almost ended disastrously in a huge pothole. I was looking to the side when I hit this foot-deep crater, and boy, did it send the bike and me down fast. Luckily the traffic had moved ahead of me at that moment, so I wasn't flattened by a cab or truck. But the lesson is simple: Stay alert. I know it gets nerve-wracking, but concentration, along with a well-honed bunny hop, is the key to bypassing, or overcoming, urban obstacles.

To help keep cars off your case, wear bright-colored clothes. A garish neon helmet cover is a good place to start. On overcast days, wear a reflective sash or vest. And just as in road touring, try to ride no earlier than an hour after sunrise and no later than an hour before sunset, so you are more visible to drivers. Of course, with work hours what they are, dawn and dusk riding are more the norm in an urban setting. If you have to ride in low light on metropolitan streets, make sure you have relectors in both wheels, on your headset, and somewhere on the seatstays. Also use a head- or handlebar-mounted light and wear a reflective vest or sash over your normal riding clothes.

Do not listen to a portable radio or tape recorder while riding. You have to be attuned to what's going on around you, traffic-wise and insult-wise.

Besides, what's the good of urban riding if you don't get a few insults to share with friends?

Do not try to emulate bicycle messengers. Yes, they are cool. Yes, they ride fast. Yes, they ride dangerously and aggressively. But then they're young, foolish, and getting paid according to how fast they complete their deliveries. Err on the side of caution when riding the canyons of steel.

Lastly, carry a weapon. No, not a gun—a Kryptonite or Gorilla lock. Why? Witness the conversation I had with a cabby in New York City a few years ago:

Me, from the back of the cab: "Hey, you sure gave that bike messenger a lot of space on that turn. Good job."

Cabby: "Yeah, well, if you'd have seen what one of those guys did to my cab with one of them horseshoe-shaped locks, you'd know why. I cut the bikey off and he bashed my cab good. Cost me two hunnert fifty bucks to get it fixed. I stay away from them bike riders."

A smile and a little courtesy are often your best defensive riding weapons.

Car racks make bike transport safer and easier.

11

Transport

Among the great inventions of modern times, the car-top "sport rack" carrier ranks right up there with the VCR and the microwave oven. A couple of quick changes, and your rack turns from a ski rack to a sailboard carrier to a kayak rack to a bike hauler. Car-top carriers are a must, especially if you drive a compact car and like to haul your recreational toys around with you.

As you'll see when you shop for one, there are sport racks for every type of car, with or without rain gutters. Besides roof racks, there are racks designed for car trunks and for rear and front bumpers. Stick with the roof rack for convenience, safety (I've seen bikes squashed in front- and rear-enders), and proven dependability.

Over the past decade, many different sport rack designs have appeared, including ones that held the entire bike, wheels and all. On these racks, bikes were never very firmly attached and tended to sway wildly as you drove. I owned one of those racks once, and although my bike never fell off the car roof, I was always anxiously anticipating the big crash.

The best sport rack design, and the one used by both top rack manufacturers, Yakima and Thule, features a quick-release skewer that holds the front fork to the rack's front crossbar and a long metal trough that encases the rear wheel. A plastic strap and buckle system, much like those used on alpine ski boots, is used to hold the rear wheel snug in the trough.

This arrangement seats the bike solidly on the rack. You can purchase as many bicycle carrier components as you want, and while two bikes seems the most practical number to carry on top of a compact car, we often get four (two with handlebars facing front, two with them facing back) on a friend's geriatric Audi two-door sedan.

Since the front tire has to be removed in order to fit the fork into the

Three up, and plenty of trunk room for the front wheels.

quick-release skewer holder, you have to store the wheel someplace. Both Yakima and Thule make wheel holders that attach to the rack's crossbars. Me, I like to store wheels in the trunk or the back seat.

Any car-top carrier rack loaded down with bicycles will cause drag on the car. You never realize how much drag until you check your gas mileage on a long trip—it's always a little shocking. To help alleviate some of the drag, rack manufacturers sell fairings that attach to the front crossbar of the rack assembly. The plastic fairing helps sweep air up over the bikes, to create a slightly better airfoil. They work, as I found out in several tests, and help improve gas mileage.

On the road, security is a continual problem. Let's say you want to stop at Monty's Chili Palace for some grits but are scared to leave the bikes unattended atop the car. Later you need some sleep and you pull into a motel. Tired, you say the hell with unpacking, and instead of bringing the bikes into your room, you leave them on the car.

If you plan to travel to great mountain biking places, make sure the car-top rack you buy is a locking one, meaning that it secures tightly to the car. Such a rack is impossible to undo and remove without a crowbar and a lot of noise accompanying the operation.

Next, invest in the security lock available from the rack's manufacturer. These locks attach to the rack and have a long cable that can be strung through the bike frames, rear wheels, and the rack's crossbars. I'd also suggest individual cable locks (purchased at any specialty bike shop) attached to each bike.

When I'm traveling alone, I employ the out-of-sight-out-of-mind security rule. I remove the front and rear wheels from my bike and store them, along with the frame, in the trunk of my car. That way no one knows if I have a bike along for the ride. (Also my mileage picks up, not having a car-top carrier breaking the wind.)

Trunk storage is possible in almost all compact cars. I drive a Mazda compact and have no trouble getting all 22 inches of my Otis bike into the trunk. A word of caution, though: the bike frame fits snugly only after the seatpost has been removed or lowered until the saddle is flush with the top tube.

Speaking of saddles, I always remove mine when I put my bike on a car-top carrier. Why? Simply because if it rains or snows or there's a dust storm or it's 120 degrees out there, the saddle doesn't get damaged. I also think a saddle sticking up in the air makes for more wind resistance, but don't ask for hard data.

Maybe I'm too fussy, but I also take the water bottles out of their cages and remove the pump. After all, who knows—they may fly off somewhere along the road, particularly if that road is bumpy. The only problem I've had with a car-top carrier was on an extremely rutted desert back road. The quick-release

It's wise to secure your racked bikes with a cable lock.

In good weather or bad, it's also wise to transport bikes with the saddles off.

Fork mounts such as these allow bike transport by pickup truck.

skewer wasn't tightened properly, and after 5 miles of bumping along, it bent, and my bike toppled onto the car's roof.

The skewer was easily hammered back to horizontal, and it held the bike wihout any further problems after I tightened it. To be on the safe side, though, keep at least one extra quick-release skewer in the trunk or glove compartment because when they get rusty, they are hard to adjust and close.

We've talked car tops, but there are thousands of truck drivers who ride mountain bikes. I'm not talking about long-haul big-rig semi drivers, but pickup devotees. There are special carriers designed to fit into the head of a pickup bed. These carriers hold the front fork in place with a quick-release skewer that is mounted on a post a foot or more off the base of the bed or on a fixture a few inches above the bed. After securing the front fork to the quick-release, the frame is stabilized with straps that attach to either the frame or the seatpost and to each side of the truck.

Securing a bike safely to a pickup bed for those times when you leave it to go shopping or to work can be a challenge. Many pickup owners drill a hole in each of the truck sidewalls and string a cable lock through those holes. Others take the bike out of the bed and, using a cable lock, secure it to the truck's front or rear axle or frame. Still others, after removing the bike's front wheel, manage to fit everything into the cab and lock it. So far, there's no definitive anti-theft device for bikes kept in pickup beds, but no doubt the manufacturers will come up with one soon.

A Gallery of
Transport Arrangements

A typical van rack.

Roof and rear racks.

An Elvis-era cruiser.

12

Getaways

Once you've become a mountain biking fanatic, you'll find that it's difficult to imagine a vacation trip that doesn't include a long multi-day tour, or day tours around a resort area, or evening rides that break up long driving days. Riding a mountain bike is the ideal way to get to know a town or a region, its unique features, its people. Astride a fat-tire bike, you'll feel all vestiges of being just another carbound tourist disappear.

THE PICK OF THE PACK

There are some incredible places to become a mountain bike tourist, and at the risk of offending a few communities, I offer my magnificent seven American fat-tire touring locales:

1. Moab, Utah
2. Crested Butte, Colorado
3. Lake Tahoe, California
4. Central Oregon
5. Durango, Colorado
6. Mammoth Lakes, California
7. Marin County, California

With the exception of Marin County, which has experienced a backlash against mountain bikes on trails, all of these places are mountain biking paradises with a variety of riding options, lots of riders, and locals who like mountain bikers and their business.

175

The best time to experience a Colorado Rocky
Mountain high? Arguably, in the fall.

Moab, Utah

Moab is a town in love with mountain biking. It's also close by some of the most satisfying riding in the world. Riding the slickrock, touring the canyons, climbing into the La Sal mountains, one discovers that this area has an unequaled variety of terrain and unparalleled vistas.

For anyone interested in early Indian cultures, geology, a little technical rock climbing, or maybe a day of river rafting along with fat-tire touring, Moab is the place. March through May and September through November are the best times to ride here, and the annual Fat Tire Festival in October (see Chapter 17) is the highlight of the riding season.

F. A. Barnes and Tom Kuehne's *Canyon Country Mountain Biking* (Moab: Canyon Country Publications, 1988) and Todd Campbell's *Beyond Slickrock* (Moab: Rim Tour Publications, 1988) are excellent guides to Moab riding. (Both, along with the *Moab Area Mountain Bike Routes* map, can be obtained from Rim Cyclery, 94 West 1st North, Moab, UT 84532.) Campbell's title makes a point. Most people come to this southwestern Utah community just to ride the famed Slickrock Trail, but believe me, it is only the hors d'oeuvre before an incredible feast of tours.

Crested Butte, Colorado

Head east a few hundred miles, then jog north, and you're in Crested Butte, Colorado. The reasons why this town attracts mountain bike riders are simple: It is, despite the influx of developers, still a pretty funky old mining community. And the single-track riding in the surrounding mountains is superb. It's Rocky Mountain riding at its best.

The riding season runs from June through October, but I suggest making a pilgrimage here in September, when the aspens turn yellow and the warm days and cool nights of Indian Summer start, making the good rides even more memorable.

It's gotten so that *not* having a mountain bike in Crested Butte marks you as an oddity, or as someone off the last tour bus. To find out more about Crested Butte, read Jeff Anderson's *Mountain Biker's Guide to Crested Butte* (self published, 1988) and the companion *Crested Butte Bike Trail Map*. (Both are available from Bicycles Etc., Box 813, Crested Butte, CO 81224.)

On the Slickrock Trail—just one of the hundreds of incredible rides available in southern Utah.

Lake Tahoe, California

Let's head west to California and Nevada, where there is superb riding in the Tahoe basin. Mountains surround the lake, and the variety of riding includes everything from logging and mining road tours to long single-track tours and cross-country rambles above the timberline. To list all the rides is impossible; to say they are the equal of those in Moab and Crested Butte would not be stretching a point.

What distinguishes Tahoe area riding are the huge granite boulders and domes, the high alpine lakes and meadows, and the forests of stately old-growth timber. Riding here is best from June through October, and unlike Crested Butte, where you're gasping for air at elevations above 9,000 feet, at Tahoe you're riding more in the less-lung-busting 6,000-to-9,000-foot range.

A must ride is the "flume ride" on the east (Nevada) side of the lake. There are two versions, intermediate and advanced, and both take you down an old flume trail cut into the granite, in many places overlooking azure Lake Tahoe.

More information on Tahoe area rides is found in Bob Ward's *Mountain Biking in the Northern Sierra* (Sacramento: Bobo Productions, 1990), which can be obtained by writing to Box 19815, Sacramento, CA 95819, or by calling Mountain Bikes and Skis Unlimited in Truckee for a copy of their *Tahoe Fat Tire Festival* book, which includes descriptions of fifteen rides.

California's northern Sierra: land of solid granite, big timber, and roaring rivers.

Central Oregon

Northwest of the Tahoe basin, the Central Oregon area around the town of Bend offers a unique year-round riding experience. This is high desert country, a designation that bears some explanation.

Say high desert and people immediately think of a rattlesnake-infested, cactus-covered, forbidding, arid landscape. Not so, the high desert. Here you have a rugged landscape dotted with junipers, sage, and lava rock outcrops at elevations over 3,000 feet. Deer, coyote, marmot, and a few rattlesnakes are the primary land inhabitants, and raptors (eagle, buzzard, and hawk) rule the skies. It's in the high desert that central Oregon fat-tire fanatics do their winter riding.

In the spring, summer, and fall, these fanatics turn west and head into the Cascades to ride the labyrinth of logging roads and single-track trails. As the summer days grow hotter and the lower elevation trails more sandy, the riders move up into the high lake district.

In central Oregon, mountain bike enthusiasts head down off the mountains in winter (left), and high into the mountains in summer (right).

The beauty of riding here is the year-long season, the variety of trails, and their proximity to Bend's (pop. 18,000) civilized amenities.

For more information on Bend and Central Oregon rides, contact Linn Moore at 2013 N.E. Patterson Circle, Bend, OR 97701, to purchase copies of his books *High Lakes Rider* and *High Desert Rider* (Bend, OR: Big Juniper Press, 1990).

Durango, Colorado

Now to southwestern Colorado for rides in the mountains of the San Juan National Forest. When the American and European mountain bike racing organizations decided to unify for a single World Mountain Bike Championship, they chose Durango as the race site. Why? Because of the variety of riding terrain, the crisp mountain air, the mountain vistas, the roaring streams, and the colorful fall foliage. Rides like the one on the Colorado Trail, which starts with 10 miles of Jeep road uphill and ends with 20 miles of downhill single-track trail back to Durango, keep riders coming back to Durango.

Apart from riding, there's first-class climbing, white-water boating, and fly fishing in the vicinity. More information on Durango area tours is available in Paul Pixler's *Hiking Trails of Southwestern Colorado* (Boulder: Pruett, 1981), Randy Jacobs's *The Colorado Trail Guidebook* (Alamosa, CO: Free Solo Press, 1988), and in *Bicycle Routes on Public Lands in Southwest Colorado* (Denver: U.S. Forest Service, 1988), a booklet prepared by the San Juan National Forest. All are available from Backcountry Experience, 780 Main Ave., Durango, CO 81301.

Mammoth Lakes and Marin County, California

We head back west to California for the last two top fat-tire touring meccas— Mammoth Lakes and Marin County: Mammoth for incredible high Sierra riding and Marin for a taste of history.

Mammoth Lakes is located on the east side of the Sierras, 300 miles from Los Angeles and 319 miles from San Francisco. The winter attraction here is skiing at Mammoth Mountain. The summer attractions are many, but topping the list is mountain biking at the ski area, out in Bodie Ghost Town (preserved but unenhanced), up to the wilderness boundary of the high Sierra country, and hundreds of other possibilities in the mountains to the north and south and the vast high desert country to the east.

Mammoth is the site of a major annual fat-tire riders gathering (see Chapter 14), and like so many other ski towns it has plenty of good accommodations and nightlife. For more information, contact the Mammoth Lakes Visitors Center at (800) 367-6572.

Last but not least, back to Marin, where the fat-tire fun all started. It's fair to say that you'd better ride Marin's trails soon, because every year local governments and park districts put more restrictions on mountain bike riding. The problem is user conflicts: conflicts between hikers, horseback riders, and fat-tire flyers.

There are speed limits for mountain bikes on many trails, and ongoing arguments over closing others to bike users. What's left to ride is impressive and a must-do. Any time of the year, a ride through the wild oaks, along the bald, windswept Marin ridges, and down into the thick forests is worth it. You can see why fat-tire riding started here. There's simply so much rolling terrain to enjoy.

For more information, contact Sunshine Cycles, 737 Center Blvd., Fairfax, CA 94930, or Sausalito Cyclery, gate 6, 1-2 Road, Sausalito, CA 94965.

UP AND COMERS

Mt. Snow, Vermont

Vermont's Mt. Snow ski area has gained a sizable biking reputation based on its network of 140 miles of trails, its guided tours, and its mountain biking school. Mt. Snow is located in southern Vermont, in the Green Mountain National Forest. More information on Mt. Snow's fat-tire riding can be obtained by calling (800) 451-4211.

For information on other Vermont rides, read William Busha's *25 Mountain Bike Tours in Vermont* (Woodstock, VT: Backcountry Publications, 1989).

A view from one of the trails that comprise the 140-mile system at Mt. Snow, Vermont.

Ridge riding in Pocahontas County, West Virginia.

Southeastern West Virginia

Perhaps America's best-kept bike touring secret is southeastern West Virginia. There are hundreds of miles of back roads and trails in the Monongahela National Forest and various state parks, offering what one local calls "a combination of New England and western U.S. riding."

The center of riding activity is Pocahontas County, part of the Potomac Highlands hard by the Allegheny Mountains. At elevations between 2,000 and 5,000 feet, riders can take up to five-day-long inn-to-inn tours. There's also a mountain biking school at The Elk River Touring Center, and an annual fat-tire festival. For more information on the place that's "like New England sixty years ago," call (304) 572-3771 or write Gil and Mary Willis at Elk River for a copy of their book *Mountain Bike Rides in Pocahontas County* (Lewisburg, WV: Roadrunner Press, 1989). The address is simply Slatyfork, WV 26291.

Crystal Mountain and Methow Valley, Washington

In the Pacific Northwest, Washington's Crystal Mountain and Methow Valley both attract fat-tire rider attention. Crystal Mountain is yet another alpine ski area that's put time and money into mountain bike trail development. The resort has 25 miles of marked trails, and an added bonus are the hundreds of miles of trails throughout the surrounding Snoqualmie National Forest. If you like your views filled with tall timber and featuring a volcano, this is your place—Crystal Mountain borders on Mt. Rainier National Park.

North and east in the Okanogan National Forest, the Methow Valley offers some of the best fat-tire inn-to-inn touring you'll find anywhere. The inns, linked by roads and cross-country ski trails, are only part of the treat here. There are also excellent mountain logging roads and trail rides in the Cascades, near the North Cascades National Park.

For information on Crystal Mountain, call (206) 663-2265. For information on the Methow Valley, call Winthrop Mountain Sports at (509) 996-2886.

The Intermountain West

In what's called the intermountain west, the Ketchum/Sun Valley, Idaho, area is noted for first-class rides close to town, plus superb rides in the Sawtooth Mountain country, north over the Galena Summit. The mountain country is the headwaters of the "River of No Return," the Salmon, and encompasses day and extended tours in the Sawtooth, Boulder, White Cloud, and Salmon River mountains. Lynne Stone's *Adventures in Idaho's Sawtooth Country* (Seattle: The Mountaineers, 1990) covers sixty-three trips for hikers and mountain bikers and is available from The Mountaineers, 306 Second Avenue West, Seattle, WA 98119.

Stanley Basin, Idaho, near the headwaters of the "River of No Return," the Salmon.

TOURS DE FORCE

Beyond day and overnight tours there are multi-day grand tours. One of the most exceptional long tours is the three-to-four-day, 96-mile ride on the White Rim trail near Moab, Utah. The trail begins and ends at the Island-in-the-Sky plateau of Canyonlands National Park, and all but 26 miles of it are within the park. The trail leads you around buttes, past Windgate sandstone ridges, down dry gulches to waypoints overlooking the park's Needles and Maze sections. The trail also passes through Stillwater and Labyrinth Canyons on the Green River. *Canyon Country Mountain Biking* (see Moab, above) covers the trail in detail.

The Flint-Land of Standing Rocks trail is another Moab multi-day tour (three to four days). The trail is marked and leads to the Standing Rocks (natural obelisks strewn about the landscape) and to a place called the Doll House. This is a great tour for letting your imagination wander, as you conjure up wild images that the rock formations create. This trail is also covered in detail in *Canyon Country Mountain Biking*.

The latest addition to the list of Moab area grand tours is Kokopelli's trail—actually a composite of many trails—which links Grand Junction, Colorado, and Moab. It's 118 miles long, over easy to moderate terrain, and has been done in a day—but for esthetic reasons, the tour should be stretched out over three to five days. For information on this ride, contact Rim Tours at (801) 259-5333.

The other long-distance multi-day tour worth investigating is the 470-mile Colorado Trail from Denver to Durango (or vice-versa, but who'd want to end an epic ride in a city?). The ride is covered in detail in Jacobs's *The Colorado Trail Guidebook* (see Durango, above).

For information on rides in the Four Corners area of Arizona, Colorado, New Mexico, and Utah, read Michael McCoy's *Mountain Bike Adventures in the Four Corners Region* (Seattle: The Mountaineers, 1990).

UP AND COMERS ACROSS THE BORDERS

Canada

Think majestic mountain ranges, and the Canadian Rockies—noted for world-class skiing, climbing, and mountaineering—come to mind. Now mountain biking has begun to flourish in the Rockies, and if you're looking for spectacular

The great American Southwest: full of grand tours yet to be discovered.

mountain scenery, wild-game-watching from the bike, waterfalls, and wild-flower-covered alpine meadows, pack up the car and head for Banff, Jasper, or Lake Louise.

Canada's Park Service allows mountain biking on designated trails in Jasper, Yoho, Banff, and Kootenay National Parks. You have to check at each park's visitor center for information on which trails are open, but the opportunities are there.

The center of Rockies riding is Banff, Canada's quintessential mountain town. From Banff you can ride trails near town or in the National Park, or you can drive a short distance to Yoho or Kootenay Park. East of Banff there are unlimited possibilities in Kananaskis Country, a 1,650-square-mile recreational area that includes three Provincial Parks: Bow Valley, Bragg Creek, and Peter Lougheed.

Also part of Kananaskis Country is the Canmore Nordic Centre. Above the town of Canmore, the Centre was the site of the 1988 Winter Olympics cross-country ski events. Since '88, the cross-country race trails have been open to mountain bike riders in the summer. The trails challenge your skills with long uphill climbs and fast downhill plunges.

Northwest of Canmore is Jasper National Park and the town of Jasper. There are dozens of good local rides in the surrounding mountains, and memorable backcountry rides in the remoter regions of the park. However, there's a problem here, and that's the fact that Jasperites refuse to wear helmets. Why? Is it to make sure people see their hairdos, or is it to show people how crazy they are? Whatever the reason, defy the local trend and save your head—and your life.

Canada's other mountain bike mecca is Whistler, in British Columbia. This ski-area town, a two-hour drive north of Vancouver, is bounded by Garibaldi Provincial Park to the east and by the Coast Mountain range to the west. To be in Whistler in summer without a mountain bike is like being at the beach in Santa Monica without a bathing suit. You stand out. Mountain bikes are beyond trendy here—they are a necessity, even if you only ride to the village for a cup of espresso at an open-air cafe.

You can take a lift up to the top of Blackcomb Mountain and ride down the alpine ski trails, or you can explore hundreds of logging and mining roads and single-track trails in the area. Get up high enough and you can make your way, cross-country, along the ridge tops from lake basin to lake basin.

For more information on Banff, Jasper, or Lake Louise, call (800) 661-8888. This puts you in contact with Alberta Tourism, where there are experts on every facet of travel and recreation in the province. Kananaskis Country information may be obtained by writing Kananaskis Country, Suite 412, 1011 Glenmore Trail, S.W., Calgary, Alberta T2V 4R6, Canada. The Canmore Nordic Centre's address is Box 1979, Canmore, Alberta T0l 0M0, Canada. For Parks Canada information, call (403) 292-4401. For Whistler information, write to the Whistler Recreation Association, Box 1400, Whistler, B.C. V0N 1B0, Canada.

Mexico

Across our southern border, Mexico is just being discovered by mountain bike riders. There are unconfirmed reports of routes being charted in the mountains of Baja California and on the Yucatan peninsula.

Routes definitely have been charted in the massive Barranca del Cobre (Copper Canyon) in the state of Chihuahua in northwest Mexico. The canyon, literally six canyons, covers over 10,000 square miles and could easily engulf America's Grand Canyon. Rugged trails and roads link canyon towns and villages. There's also a main railway line that skirts along the edges of this canyon country, which mountain biking fanatics can use for transport to different riding areas.

For more on Barranca del Cobre, contact the Mexican Government Tourism Office, 10100 Santa Monica Blvd., Room 224, Los Angeles, CA 90067.

TOURING COMPANIES

Traditionally, bicycle touring companies have offered guided road-bike tours. However, today many are also offering mountain bike tours, or use mountain bikes as their main mode of on- and off-road transportation. These companies' tour offerings vary from year to year; write to them for more information.

Backcountry Bicycle Tours, P.O. Box 4029, Bozeman, MT 59772

Backroads, 1516 Fifth Street, Berkeley, CA 94710-2573

Rim Tours, 94 West 1st North, Moab, UT 84532

Slickrock Adventures, P.O. Box 1400, Moab, UT 84532

Vermont Bicycle Tours, Box 711, Bristol, VT 05443

Vermont Country Cyclers, P.O. Box 145, Waterbury, VT 05677

Vermont Mountain Bike Tours, Box 526, Pittsfield, VT 05672

Bike tour companies usually provide inn-to-inn services and other amenities to minimize hassles and maximize touring pleasure.

RESOURCES

Contact Latitude 40°, P.O. Box 4086, Boulder, CO 80306 for trail maps of the following areas: Boulder City, Colorado; Crystal Basin (Tahoe National Forest), California; El Dorado National Forest, California; Marin and Sonoma counties, California; and the Slickrock Trail, Utah.

The mountain bike is no longer just an American fun machine.

13

Beyond North America

Riding a mountain bike in Europe five years ago, you would have drawn stares in the north and would have had to answer a torrent of questions in the south. Today mountain bikes are known and accepted throughout the Continent, and in fact have become popular recreational vehicles.

For some years Europe has been a popular choice for Americans making a grand road-bike tour. And while it's doubtful that area bike shops and bicycle touring outfits will soon be offering mountain bike tours and touring gear, a mountain bike, fitted with slick tires, is ideal for European road touring. It's stable, and when you get on some of those narrow, heavily trafficked roads, fat tires make it easy to ride in the dirt or gravel on the road's shoulder.

If you decide to use your mountain bike for European road touring, I'd recommend adding bar-ends or triathlon bars to give you another, more relaxing, position on the handlebars. On any long tour you'll want to stretch out and change hand positions. Staying in the same riding position for a long time makes you cramp up and takes a lot of the enjoyment out of the touring experience.

If your tour will be an on- and off-road affair, however, use knobby tires instead of slicks, and make the bar extension(s) an optional add-on. And for any partially or completely off-road tour, be prepared by taking along additional parts that might be difficult to find locally: a section of chain to repair breaks, several tubes, brake and shifter cable, spare spokes, a spare rear derailleur, and a spare set of tires along with your normal repair kit. For the spare tires, take Kevlar bead tires; they fold up easily for storage in your panniers.

Also pack the best rain suit you can afford, along with light moisture-transport and insulative clothing layers (synthetic underwear, fleece sweater, jacket). When it comes to shoes, the best for foreign touring are the lug-sole low- or mid-cut models that can be worn for hiking and casual wear as well as for cycling. Now that we're equipped, let's go biking.

ENGLAND AND SCOTLAND

The British were the first people outside the U.S. to get excited about mountain bikes. If you're a keen watcher of cable television, by now you've probably seen at least one adventure show featuring a group of Brits mountain biking in the remotest parts of Africa, the Middle East, or the Far East.

Meanwhile, back in England there are thousands of miles of hiking and walking paths that are, as of this writing, open to cyclists. It's possible to ride from the south of England to the Scottish border almost entirely on trails.

The joy of mountain bike touring here is being on the footpaths and back roads, where you have the opportunity to see what remains of English village life. Then, of course, there are the quaint B and B's (bed and breakfast establishments), and the pubs with their local bitters, ales, and stouts.

If you can make only one fat-tire trip to England, I recommend that you ride in the Lake District. This is Wordsworth country, noted for its valley and fell (hill/mountain) trails, which are now seeing increasing mountain bike activity. Mountain bike rental ("hire") shops have sprung up in all major Lake District commercial centers, and you can rent a bike for as little as $70 a week. The best aspect of Lake District mountain bike riding is going inn-to-inn across the fells. That, and finishing each day at the local with a lager in hand.

To the north, you'll find Scottish mountain bike touring amiable on-road, but as tough as it gets off-road. This past October, mountain rescue units were called out to find two mountain bikers long overdue on what appeared to be an easy two-day trip. But when the winds blow and the rain falls in sheets, the trails turn to goo and the going gets rough.

Scotland has some incredible trails, such as the West Highland, which goes from Fort William to Glasgow. This trail, like most in Scotland, is rough, rocky, and often ankle-deep in mud. Scottish weather makes off-road mountain biking here a hard go. But if you want spectacular settings, magical light for photography, and a happy challenge, then head to the highlands.

I've ridden in the mountains surrounding Fort William, including sections of trail on Ben Nevis, Britain's highest peak. Farther inland, there are trails in the Cairngorms that can be ridden in one day or in multi-day trips.

One of my favorite rides is around Loch Rannoch and up into one of the last remaining vestiges of the ancient old-growth Caledonian Forest. From

Loch Rannoch Station you can also cross Rannoch Moor (a day trip) and arrive in time for the evening opening of the Climber's Pub at the King's Cross Hotel. Pub regulars may talk of encounters with the Egg-Faced Man of Rannoch Moor. He's been out there for years, scaring the wits out of locals but judiciously avoiding tourists on foot and bicycle.

SCANDINAVIA

The greatest mountain biking assets in Norway, Sweden, and Finland are their thousands of miles of cross-country ski trails. I've skied in each country several times, but had the chance to mountain bike only in Norway. And what a treat that was.

Norway has a national touring association that maintains backcountry hotels and huts, prints maps and guides, and helps point you in the right direction for a great trip. Regional touring affiliates maintain information centers to help hikers, backpackers, and now mountain bikers.

Norwegian fat-tire touring is, for the most part, a combination of riding and hiking. Often trails are too rough, rutted, rocky, muddy, or just plain tough for riding. So you hike and push, hike and carry. But it's worth it, for the mountain views are superb and the facilities as comfortable or as rustic as you want.

Norway's backcountry accommodations are divided into four categories: mountain hotels, mountain huts, self-service huts, and emergency huts. Each serves a distinct purpose and clientele.

The mountain hotel can be reached by car and usually sits on the boundary of a national park or wilderness area. Here you get three meals a day, a nice room, and entertainment (of a low-key variety in keeping with the setting), for about $75 per night for two.

A mountain hut is actually a hotel, but a hotel that you have to hike or bike to. Once there, you stay in a private or dorm room and get two prepared meals per day (breakfast and dinner). Hut personnel will also prepare your trail lunch and fill your thermos bottle (a traditional Norwegian hiking must) with tea, coffee, or hot soup. All this for about $50 per night for two in a dorm room.

Self-service huts are comfortable unmanned huts, generally spaced about a day's hike apart on more remote trails. A typical hut has a living/dining room and private sleeping rooms (quilts on the beds). The kitchen is fully stocked with cookwear and utensils, and there's always a closet full of canned and dehydrated food for you to use. If you buy a membership in the national touring

Norway offers tidy villages and breathtaking scenery for the intrepid mountain bike tourer.

association, self-service huts cost about $36 per night for two (including food); they're more without the membership. Everything is on the honor system: At the end of your stay, you clean up the hut, tally up the number of nights stayed plus food used (a handy price list is posted on the hut wall), and put your money in a envelope and into a metal box ("Boss"). Later the local or regional touring group collects the funds during one of their restocking trips.

At the bottom end of the scale are the emergency huts, which in most cases are prefab buildings placed in the most remote locations. There are usually four beds, a table and chairs, plates and utensils, a camp stove, and fuel. As the name indicates, they are to be used for emergencies or when you get caught between self-service or mountain huts. There's no charge.

I've toured hut-to-hut on Norway's wet west coast in a region called the Stolsheimen. This high, treeless area, cut into a rolling landscape by ancient glacial activity, was the Norwegian resistance movement's stronghold from which they harassed the Nazis during World War II. Topo maps of the Stolsheimen date from the war and carry the legend (in Norse) "Prepared by the U.S. Army." A tour here is as tough as it gets.

For more relaxed bike and hike touring, I suggest Rondane National Park, near Lillehammer. Dirt service roads lead to the mountain huts, and from there you can ride or hike off into the wilds on day or multi-day trips. Rondane is Norway's first national park. The mountains are rounded, the lowlands glaciated smooth. It's the place of Norwegian folk legend, with Peer Gynt's hut nestled in the verdant landscape.

Close by, around Lillehammer (site of the 1992 Winter Olympics), there are hundreds of miles of cross-country ski trails to ride. For history buffs, a ride on the Birkebeiner Trail is a must.

The Birkebeiners (literally "birch legs," for their birch-bark leggings) were soldiers who in 1206 saved the infant Haakon Haakson, future king of Norway, by carrying him on skis over the Dovre mountains to safety. It's the Bonnie Prince Charlie story gone north, with skiers substituted for rowers.

There's no substitute for Norway's Jotunheimen Mountains, a range of jagged alpine peaks, glaciers, and year-round snow-capped summits. As with every wild Norwegian area, the Jutenheimen is laced with trails and service roads and dotted with huts. The riding/hiking experience is about as close as you can come to being in the Alps without being there.

And perhaps the closest thing to the world's best urban area riding has to be in Nordmarka, in Oslo. Nordmarka is a huge forest preserve laced with 1,500 kilometers of cross-country ski trails. There are also walking, hiking, and cycling trails, so there's plenty of variety. There are huts and hotels in Nordmarka, so you can do point-to-point touring. Or you can stay in downtown Oslo, take your bike on the tram up to the Holmenkollen station, and then ride off into Nordmarka.

WESTERN EUROPE

Mountain biking in the alpine countries (France, Italy, Austria, Switzerland) has been, until very recently, a downhill experience. Using *téléfériques,* trams, or chair lifts, riders got a lift up with their bikes, then rode downhill.

As mountain bike riding has become more popular, more alpine riders are branching out, finding trails in the foothills of the Alps or riding in the lower, more rounded mountain ranges like the Pyrenees and the Jura.

A sign on the trail in France's Midi. There are times when you'll long for a set of the incredible spiked tires shown here.

France's Jura mountains, for example, run along the Swiss border and at their northern end touch on Germany. Astride your VTT (*vélo de tout terrain*, or all-terrain bicycle), you can ride roads and trails from *gîte* to *gîte*. (A *gîte* is a cross between a bed-and-breakfast and a hostel, and they feature hearty local meals. The typical breakfast is a glass of wine, hard smoked sausage, cheese, and rough bread. A great way to start a cycling day.)

Apart from the Jura, France maintains the most extensive network of footpaths in the world—some 30,000 kilometers (18,000 miles) of them. That's a lot of trails through such spectacular and easy riding areas as the Dordogne, in the southwest, and Brittany, in the north.

Mountain biking is just now catching on in Austria. Most of the good rides are on biking paths and logging roads at the base of the Alps. A great place to start an exploration is in St. Anton am Arlberg. This is the birthplace of modern alpine skiing, and the Tiroleans have taken to mountain biking with the same enthusiasm they have for skiing.

But it's Italy where mountain biking has taken root and grown. There you'll find outstanding riding in the mountain foothill country of the Piedmont and Venetia, the Dolomites, and in Lombardy's lake country. Italy is the scene of many fat-tire races and events, and has an official mountain bike club and organized tours (see the resources section at the end of this chapter).

Trekking the Austrian Alps the old way and the new way.

During the mild winter of 1989, my wife and I were astounded by the number of mountain bikers riding through the countryside outside Verona. Resting at a small foothills cafe, we were suddenly surrounded by a group of mud-spattered Italian mountain bikers. The scene could have been on Mt. Tamalpais in Marin County. These riders were proud of their custom bikes, and they gave me a description of the components in Italian. When they came to their tires, they blurted out in English: "Ground Controls—California." There we stood, linked in brotherhood by mountain bikes and good American rubber.

In Alba, a mountain bike shop was packed with people. The shop's top brand: Specialized. In every place we visited, even the seaport of Genoa, the mountain bike shops were doing a brisk business and the mountain bikers were out riding. As they do with so many sports, the Italians have embraced fat tires with gusto.

AUSTRALIA AND NEW ZEALAND

Down Under, mountain biking is catching on. New Zealand has long been a road rider's touring paradise, and more tourers are now using mountain bikes. Off-road touring is just opening up in New Zealand, but considering the great tracks (trekking trails)—Routeburn, Abel Tasman, and the Milford—the possibilities for backcountry hut-to-hut fat-tire touring are impressive.

Aussie mountain biking is still in its infancy, but here, too, the possibilities are endless. There are established fat-tire tours in the northwestern Tablelands, and there's informal riding in the Blue Mountains, the New England Range, and the Snowy Mountains in the southwest. There's also the great mass of South Australia, Western Australia, and the Kimberly region to be explored. Backroads Bicycle Touring will start running guided mountain bike trips to the north Queensland coast, including Daintree River National Park, in November 1991.

SOUTH AMERICA

Think of the vast expanse of Brazil, the mountains of Argentina and Chile, the rugged terrain of Patagonia and Tierra del Fuego, the llama land of Peru, the Inca trail—and you've barely touched all the possibilities of South American mountain bike travel. South America has the potential of becoming the mountain biker's Eden.

In 1988 Kevin Mireles, of Whittier, California, spent $10\frac{1}{2}$ months riding throughout South America. A year later he spent four months riding in Argentina and Chile. "It sounds trite," Mireles says, "but the possibilities are endless. The best all-around riding is in Chile and Argentine and Patagonia, but if you want some incredible long downhill rides, I'd head to Peru and Chile."

Mireles was a pioneer. On each return trip he reports seeing hundreds more mountain bikers throughout South America and brings back stories of great rides—such as in the mountains near Rio and the mountains of Venezuela. Obviously South America is the place for fat-tire exploration.

In the foothills of the Andes.

THE EXOTICS

Tibet, Bali, Nepal, Papua New Guinea, China. Except for Tibet, which is currently off-limits to foreign travel, these are the countries that have seen increased mountain bike travel during the past several years. The rides are difficult and generally made by organized tour groups.

A typical exotic tour is the twenty-one-day Off The Deep End Travels tour in Papua New Guinea. During the first week, the tour covers the 60-mile Kokoda Trail, between Port Moresby and Kokoda. This native trading trail switchbacks through the mountains, rising and falling 20,000 feet during the week. After a break for snorkeling at the seaside, cyclists fly to the starting point for a ride over dirt roads through the Owen-Stanley Range, in incredible jungle country.

Fat-tire touring in Bali.

To read Bali's road signs it might be wise to bone up on the native language.

PACKING UP

There are two ways to ship your bike abroad: in a box or in a specially made bike case. The problem with each is how to store it once you get to your destination.

Storage can be a chore because in less-traveled areas of the world, air

Packing Up

A mountain bike properly broken down for travel. Note the handlebars taped to the top tube and the wood block at the front fork dropouts. Don't pack the cat by mistake.

Once you've boxed your bike, seal it with reinforced tape and secure it further with old inner tubes. As you can see, the boxes can be used more than once—this one has been opened.

A sturdy nylon carrying bag will handle hauling your bike, provided you pad the frame and wheels with foam or extra clothing.

terminal or train depot storage facilities (common in Europe) are not available. Nor are storage lockers. What to do? I suggest spending your first night at a good hotel and seeing if they will store your box or case until you return. If they can't, they should be able to direct you to a place or person who can provide storage.

But how to ship the bike abroad? Obviously the hard-shell cases protect your bike the best. That's their plus side. The minus side is that they are expensive and generally hold little more than just the bike. Using a standard bike box (your local bicycle specialty sells them) works fine, and you can pad the bike with clothing. A box, however, is hard to lug around and store.

The last option, and the one I've used, is the padded bike bag. Made of rugged nylon, most bike carrier bags look like a large envelope. They zip open to reveal a main storage compartment for the frame and inner side sleeves that hold the wheels. Carrier bags have sewn-on grips and a shoulder carrying strap. They are lightweight, easy to haul, and can be loaded down with clothes for extra padding. In fact, the smart traveler will make sure that all his clothes, panniers, and so forth fit in the bike carrier bag so he doesn't need to take along much more than a small rucksack on the plane.

Before booking any flight, check on the airline's fee for carrying a bicycle. Many international airlines require advance notice that you're taking a bike. Others don't and, I've found, often pass the bike through without charge. This usually happens when the ticket agent is harried and they're waving things through to speed up the check-in process. But rather than trust to luck, I'd check in advance.

SELLING YOUR BIKE ABROAD

When mountain bikes were new and exotic, those who took them abroad were always getting offers for them. The possibility still exists, because better American bikes have that panache that status seekers crave. I wouldn't count on selling my bike to pay for my passage back home, but I should think that unless you've developed a passion for your machine, it is marketable on foreign soil. And if it's a one-of-a-kind bike or a well-known top-end brand, not only will its resale value be greater but so will the likelihood of its being stolen.

RESOURCES

England and Scotland

Lake District National Park Authority
Park Management and Visitor Services
National Park Office, Brockhole
Windermere, Cumbria LA23 1LJ,
  England

Transcotland Holiday Expeditions
216 Newhaven Rd.
Edinburgh, EH6 4QE, Scotland

Norway

Den Norske Turisforening
Postboks 1963 Vika
N-0125 Oslo 1, Norway

France

MAPS

Institut Géographique National (IGN)
107 Rue La Boétie
75008 Paris, France

JURA

Pierre Jouille
Gîte d'Etape
Grand-Mont 25790
Les Gras, France

Austria

St. Anton am Arlberg Information
Tourism Office
A-6580 St. Anton am Arlberg,
Austria

Italy

Mountain Bike Club of Italy
Via Durini 24
Milan, Italy

THREE-DAY TOURS

Ulisse Sport
Strade regionale 32
11013 Courmayeur (AO), Italy

Europe (general)

Europeds
883 Sinex Ave.
Pacific Grove, CA 93950

Australia

Australian Tourist Commission
2121 Avenue of the Stars,
  Suite 1200
Los Angeles, CA 90067

Backroads Bicycle Touring
1516 Fifth St.
Berkeley, CA 94710

New Zealand

Backcountry Bicycle Tours
P.O. Box 4029
Bozeman, MT 59772

South America

Power Tours
10581 Rancho Rd.
La Mesa, CA 92041

The Exotics

BALI

Backroads Bicycle Touring
1516 Fifth St.
Berkeley, CA 94710

PAPUA NEW GUINEA

Off The Deep End Travels
Box 7511
Jackson, WY 83001

TIBET/CHINA

Boojum Expeditions
Box 223
Leucadia, CA 92024

NEPAL

Wilderness Travel
801 Allston Way
Berkeley, CA 94710

Reading Matter

There are a number of good mountain biking publications in Europe and the Southern Hemisphere. A partial list follows:

Mountain Bike UK
30 The Paddock
Chatham, Kent ME4 4RE, England

Velo Vert
6 bis Avenue de la Grotte
78400 Chatou, France

Tutto Mountain Bike
Via Nino Brixio, 40
20129 Milan, Italy

Bike
Albert-Rosshaupter 73
800 Munich 70, Germany

Australian Cyclist
GPO Box 272
Sydney, NSW, Australia 2001

Mountain Bike New Zealand
P.O. Box 31-272
Lower Hutt, New Zealand

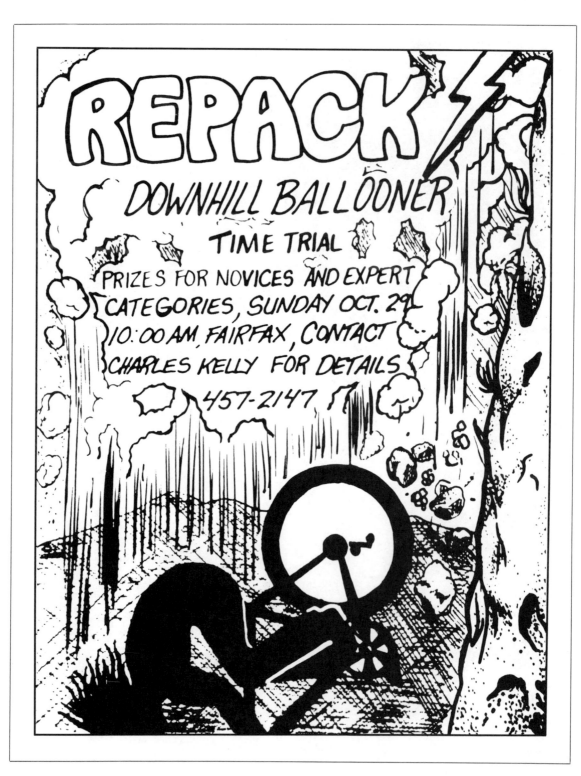

14

Races, Festivals, and Schools

It didn't take long before the original Marin County klunker riders started racing their bikes. Most of the fat-tire pioneers—Gary Fisher, Joe Breeze, Otis Guy—had been road racers. So one October day in 1976 the klunker bunch rode over to the top of a hill on Marin Municipal Water District property between San Anselmo and Fairfax and staged a downhill time-trial race. The riders raced against the clock, down a course that dropped 1,300 feet in 2.2 miles. The event was called the "Repack" because everyone had to repack their overheated coaster brake bearings with grease at the end of each descent. With Repack, mountain bike racing was born.

Meanwhile, a bit farther east, the mountain biking brigade in Crested Butte, Colorado, was staging a race of their own. After trucks had hauled participants' bikes to the top of 12,700-foot Pearl Pass (a back-roads pass to Aspen), they rode downhill, with a few ups and creek crossings, to Crested Butte.

"We heard about the Crested Butte event," says original Repacker Charles Kelly, "and we decided to head out there the next year to see what was up."

The Marin riders arrived in Crested Butte in September 1977 and immediately convinced the locals that the cool deal would be to ride from Crested Butte over Pearl Pass to Aspen. Everyone took two days, with Jeeps and pickups carrying the food and camping gear, to make the 40-mile trip. The tour, and the week of riding around Crested Butte, was so successful that the Marin riders decided to come back the next year. They did, and Fat Tire Week was born: a week of touring and racing, capped off with the Pearl Pass tour during the height of the fall colors.

By 1979 the idea of racing mountain bikes had captured the imagination of other Californians, and informal races began springing up all around the

Mountain bike racing originated—where else—in Marin County in 1976, when the first Repack was run.

Old-time Repack style as demonstrated by Gary Fisher.

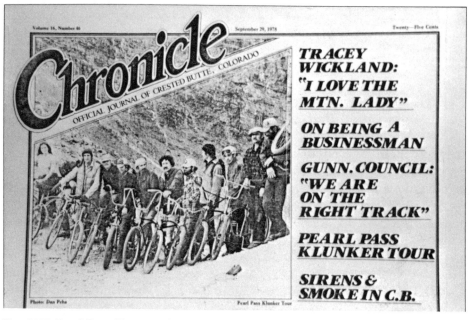

The 1978 Pearl Pass Tour was front-page news.

state. Some of this enthusiasm spread north to Oregon and east to Colorado.

The period from 1979 to 1983 is now considered the golden age of mountain bike racing, the time of loosely organized long-distance point-to-point races with few rules and the unspoken yet understood credo that surviving the ride and having fun was more important than winning. An outlaw atmosphere surrounded the events, and there was always a rip-roaring post-race party.

The grand classics, the must-do's, were California's Whiskeytown Downhill near Redding, the Rockhopper in Santa Rosa, the Bidwell Bump in Chico, the Reseda To The Sea in southern California, and the Central Coast Klunker Classic. To the north, there was Oregon's Revenge of the Siskiyous and the Cascade Cruise.

Soon events became more organized and formalized, with racers putting more emphasis on winning. Manufacturers started to sponsor events and teams, and in January 1983 a group of racers, event promoters, and riders met at Charles Kelly's Marin County home and formed the National Off-Road Bicycle Association (NORBA). NORBA's first leader was southern California fireman Glenn O'Dell.

An avid off-road fat-tire tourer, O'Dell saw NORBA's main goal as preserving access to backcountry trails and, hopefully, access to wilderness areas. However, as the organization grew, it became more concerned with organizing and promoting races.

The Marin riders at Crested Butte in 1978. A fine time was had by all.

Fat-tire touring's first (and still going strong) journalist, Charlie Kelly, "repacking." Note the ensemble: jeans, engineer boots, work gloves.

NORBA created a national point series race championship, a national championship, and a world championship. As the number of races grew, they spelled the end of many of the grand classics because their organizers lost interest when formality replaced informality.

Today there are more circuit races and lap races, more professional riders, more sponsored teams, and more emphasis on equipment. There are four competition classes for both men and women: juniors (age 16 to 17), seniors (18 to 34), veterans (35 to 44), and masters (45 and up). There are also four category classes: beginner, sport (intermediate competitor), expert, and pro/elite. People in the last class are sponsored professional riders who race for cash purses.

All competitors pay $25 a year for a racing license or, if they race only once or twice a year, $5 per race. The competitor's card fee helps NORBA insure, promote, and organize the events. For more information, contact NORBA at 1750 E. Boulder St., Colorado Springs, CO 80909.

Fat Tire Week still lives, now held in July instead of September. Oregon's Revenge of the Siskiyous has also gone through a date change, from July 4th to early August, but this race still retains some of the flavor of early mountain bike racing. Colorado's Iron Horse Classic is the top race event in the Rockies, and Vermont's Mt. Snow Race has become the must-do event in the East. The last remaining big-time mass-participation races are the Mammoth Mountain Kamikaze at the Mammoth Mountain ski resort in Mammoth Lakes, California, and the Chequamegon Fat Tire Festival in Cable and Hayward, Wisconsin. Both are so popular that entries are limited to 1,500 at Mammoth and 2,250 at Chequamegon.

What makes both festivals so well attended is the variety of racing over several days. At Mammoth there are uphill, trials, and cross-country competitions, plus the famous Kamikaze downhill, which starts at the top of 11,503-foot Mammoth Mountain and descends over a steep road to the base lodge at 9,000 feet. The speeds attained on this course are astounding; the current record, held by professional John Tomac, is 5 minutes 30 seconds, or approximately 53 miles per hour.

The Chequamegon Fat Tire Festival features four events over two days, including a 40-mile cross-country race, a bike orienteering event, a criterium, and a novices ("short and fat") race. A great many riders come for the parties, which are among the Midwest's best apres-sporting-event bashes. The 1990 Chequamegon will long be remembered because three-time Tour de France and two-time World Professional Championship winner Greg LeMond was on hand. More than on hand—he won the 40-mile cross-country race and showed that class is class, no matter what type of bike or terrain.

For people who like the fun but not the competition, there are two memorable fat-tire events every year. The first, the Fat Tire Tour of Milwaukee, is held in June. The second, the Moab Mountain Bike Festival, is held during Halloween week.

The Fat Tire Tour of Milwaukee is exactly what is says it is: A throng of cyclists on every conceivable type of bike takes off to see the city and stop off at such well-known local attractions as Wolski's Tavern. After a picnic at a local park, featuring—what else—bratwurst (brats), the diehards take in a Brewers baseball game at County Stadium.

There's no baseball at Moab—only a week of organized tours through parts of the surrounding countryside, a couple of informal races, and a spectacular Halloween Day bike parade. It's worth the trip just to see the parade costumes.

Getting ready to tour at
Fat Tire Week, Crested
Butte, Colorado.

They're off and pedaling
down the main street of
Hayward, Wisconsin, at the
start of the Chequamegon 40.

Yes, that's Greg LeMond himself, at the start (left) and finish (right) of the 1990 Chequamegon 40.

Nothing but good clean fun at the annual Fat Tire Tour of Milwaukee.

For East Coast riders, the West Virginia Fat Tire festival in June is now well established. The five-day gathering includes three days of tours and clinics and two days of racing. There's plenty of camping space for attendees, and live music and good food follow each day's events.

Particulars on Moab can be obtained from Rim Cyclery, 94 West 1st North, Moab, UT 84532. Information on the Milwaukee event can be obtained by writing FTTM, 921 W. 66th St., Richfield, MN 55423. For West Virgina information, write to the Elk River Touring Center, Slatyfork, WV 26921. Chequamegon information can be obtained by calling (715) 798-3811. Mammoth information is available at (619) 934-0651. Information on all other race events is available through NORBA: 1750 E. Boulder St., Colorado Springs, CO 80909.

SO YOU WANT TO RACE

If you're interested in racing, you have to get with a training program. The idea that if you ride every day, you'll be okay for racing is false. So is the idea that if you ride super-long distances at a slow pace, you'll be race ready. Ride long and slow and you'll race slow; ride every day without a training goal and you'll never race to your potential.

There are hundreds of training programs, each with its own strengths and weaknesses. Without getting too technical (and writing an entire book), I'd say to go for quality, not quantity, and for variety, not sameness, in your training.

"Quality, not quantity" means getting the best workout every day and not just piling up lots of miles. Variety means combining long-distance rides to build endurance, interval sessions to build speed and strength, and tempo sessions to simulate race conditions.

Another key factor in any training schedule is balancing your efforts so you don't become overly proficient at, say, downhills at the expense of uphills. Try to work on each aspect of your riding, and if one area of your technique is weak, devote one or two special sessions a month to working on nothing but that.

Race training should begin in the spring, at least two months before your first race. A good way to get a training schedule started is to look over the lineup of upcoming races, pick the ones you want to point for, and build your training so that it leads up to those events.

Early on in your training schedule, work on building an endurance base. That means taking longer rides, quality rides at a higher tempo than the one you'd use if you were out touring with friends.

In mountain bike racing, true grit is a necessary intangible asset.

After a few weeks of endurance building, add interval rides twice a week, either up a long steady hill or over a short rolling course. Ride the course as hard as you can. When you finish, pedal slowly back to the starting point and do the course hard once again. Take your pulse before each start, and make a note of the rate. When your pulse rate fails to fall back down near that starting count, it's time to quit the intervals.

Intervals build cardiovascular strength and get your body used to "going under" and recovering—something that happens many times in a typical mountain bike race.

Later, as the race season draws near, add rides at race tempo. Start out quickly, as you would in a mass start, and then settle into a rhythm; punch up the hills, relax a bit on the downhills, sprint to the finish.

Overtraining is the bane of most athletes, and mountain bike racers are no different. To avoid overtraining, use the old "hard/easy" approach. Train hard one day; train easy the next. Take at least one day off every week to relax.

When the race season starts, the race day becomes your hard day for the week. After that you'll have a very easy day, a moderate day, maybe an interval day, an easy day, a rest day, and then race day again.

The importance of rest cannot be overstated. If you feel sluggish or tired, take it easy. Don't fall into the old trap of "training through" sickness or low periods. Don't think for a minute that a few more hard miles the week of a race will make you perform better. If you don't have the training base by the time the season starts, no amount of extra workout is going to help you catch up.

Another tip is to work out all the technical details you might encounter in racing before the season starts. A checklist might include: breakdowns and what to carry to repair them, clothes, pre-race diet, in-race food and drink.

You have to be prepared for mechanical failures and know how to cope with them in a race situation. Fixing a flat is mandatory. Sooner or later you'll have to fix one, so you should practice removing and replacing a tube in advance, both to make sure you have it down and and to see that you have all the right tools on board.

Having the right clothes may seem like a silly thing to work on pre-season, but it is critical. You have to have shorts that feel comfortable and protect your upper legs, you have to test several jerseys (one for cool days, one for hot days) to see if they keep you at the right temperature, you have to test headbands under your helmet to see if they absorb sweat properly to keep it from streaming down your face, you have to make sure sure your socks fit and feel perfect. Make a mental checklist of what goes into your clothes bag and review it before you leave for a race so that when you arrive at the site, everything you need is there.

To race well, you have to master the ups and downs. Here, mountain bike pioneer Tom Ritchey ascends in style.

Your diet is next, and it can save or ruin a season. Essentially a diet centered on complex carbohydrates is best; it will give you plenty of muscle endurance and power. This diet eliminates the need to carbohydrate-load before a race. Loading was once considered the best way to increase muscle sugar stores before an event, but as many good athletes have found, it didn't always work. A steady diet of complex carbohydrates plus a slight load the night before the race is the best plan. Start to diet right when you begin your training schedule. Read Covert Bailey's *Target Diet* (South Lake Tahoe: Bailey, 1983) for general dietary ground rules.

In-race food and drink can be very important if the race is long and lasts several hours. Never test athletic drinks, energy bars, or energy foods during a race. Try them out in a simulated race situation long before you ever get to a starting line. You may find, as I did, that one athletic drink makes you ill, another goes down easily; one energy bar is easy to digest and gives you energy while the other does nothing more than give you cramps.

Finally, take more rest than you think you need. As your training intensifies, take a day off and see how you feel when you get back on the bike the following day. Then try a two-day layoff and see how that feels. Always take one or two days off (don't ride; don't run; lie low) before a race.

Then comes race day. A couple of ideas for first-timers: Try to ride as much of the course as possible a few days before the race, so you'll know what to expect. If that's not possible, ride the first 2 miles prior to the start on race day. Always warm up for at least an hour prior to the start; ride easily and steadily during your warmup, and during the last ten minutes do a few hard intervals to get your heart pumping and prepared for the work ahead. Never hang around the start line, waiting for the start; get away from the milling crowd, get loose, do your intervals, and arrive at the start line a minute before the gun. Set a steady pace when the gun goes off, and don't go out too hard in your first race; instead, go for a smooth race where you start moderately fast, and safely, and build momentum for a fast finish.

When the race is over, review the high and low points you experienced, and think about how you can smooth out the rough spots in the next race. With your first race under your belt, you can start thinking about strategy, in-race feeding, how to avoid accidents, and so on. You have to race in order to understand these factors, and each race makes you more aware of what you have to do.

Strategy is tied to the kind of racer you are. Are you a fast-out-of-the-gate sprinter who goes as hard as he can and then hangs on until he collapses at the finish line? Are you a slow starter who builds momentum to a crescendo at the finish? Are you a fast starter who slows mid-race, and after seeing how much energy he has left, does an all-out sprint over the last few miles? Knowing how you best like to ride helps determine your race strategy.

If your strength is uphills, you have to save energy so you can make up time on them. If you're a downhill fanatic, you have to make sure you don't lose too much time between the downs. Push yourself hard to learn what your physical limits are, and base your race strategy on them.

Plan your in-race feeding and drinking, including when and where you should do it. Cresting a short hill is always a good place to grab a drink or munch some food, but maybe you prefer a short downhill for noshing.

Consider the near-accidents you had in your last race and figure out how to avoid them in the future. My best accident-proofing is to yell like crazy: "On your left, On your right, Move it, turkey!"—anything to let the riders ahead of me know what I'm doing and where I'm going. As with any mountain bike riding, anticipation is the key to avoiding accidents.

Self-generated accidents are easily avoided by not getting too revved up and out of control. Always maintain control over your bike, and back off when

The perennial World Champion Ned Overend (shown here at the 1987 Worlds).

you feel yourself losing control or running out of strength to control the bike.

Also consider your post-race plans. After you've checked the results board, warm down with a 15- to 30-minute ride. When you get back home—or to the motel or campsite—lie down on your back with your legs above your head. Hold them there (against a wall, tree, car), and reaching up, massage your calf and thigh muscles. Letting the blood drain out of the legs and massaging your muscles will help dissipate the lactic acid that builds up during a hard race.

My best advice is left for last: Never take racing too seriously. At its best, racing offers an opportunity for personal exploration, a chance to see what your body can do. To keep my perspective, I race under pseudonyms (The Right Reverend Lester Polyester, Art Deco, Elvis Elvis). My alter egos keep me honest. They remind me that it's all for fun.

SCHOOLS

As mountain bike riding has become more popular, so has the need for places where people can go to learn the fundamentals and the fine points. Mt. Snow, Vermont, has an official mountain bike school that offers personalized instruction (835S Mountain Rd., Mt. Snow, VT 05356). California's Otter Bar Lodge

Yo! It's Art Deco, a.k.a. the author, showing the right attitude at the World Championships.

Some racing skills, such as slalom biking, are best learned through experience.

Nota bene, students: Racing can be hard on equipment.

specializes in mountain bike holidays and bike instruction weeks (Forks of Salmon, CA 96031). And Elk River Touring Center, West Virgina, offers a "learn while doing" mountain bike program from April through October (Slatyfork, WV 26291).

ACCESS ISSUES

The International Mountain Bike Association (IMBA) is an organization that is concerned with land access issues. In many parts of the country, parks and federal lands have been closed to mountain bikes. To help prevent further closures and to keep current riding areas open, IMBA is working with federal, state, and local officials. IMBA can be reached at Route 2, Box 303, Bishop, CA 93514.

Breakdowns can occur anywhere, so knowing some basic repair techniques is a must.

15

Care and Maintenance

There are three schools of thought on bicycle care and maintenance: (1) the never-touch-the-bike school, (2) the do-the-minor-repairs-but-leave-the-majors-alone school, and (3) the do-it-all school. Adherents of the first school head down to the local specialty bike shop for help whenever the least thing goes wrong. School number two adherents keep their bikes in shape with regular tune-ups and preventive maintenance and use a bike shop for major, more technical, repairs.

Those of the last school of action believe that they should do it all, from truing wheels to installing new bearings in the bottom bracket. These diehards will tackle every repair despite, in many cases, having neither the time, skills, tools, nor inclination to do so. For some, being a qualified part-time bike mechanic is something akin to a manhood rite of passage—serious stuff. To me it seems like a lot of unnecessary trouble.

I'm of the do-the-minors, leave-the-majors-alone school, and so will address only the basics of bike repair in this chapter. There are several excellent books on bike repair on the market; a couple are listed at the end of the chapter should you want to get further into the *sturm und drang* of repair work.

TOOLS OF THE TRADE

Chain Tool. This handy tool is a must for trail use and is good to have in the general repair kit. The chain tool allows you to partially remove and reseat the pins that hold the chain links together.

Allen Key Set. Allen keys can be purchased separately or in a three-pronged star tool; 4-, 5-, and 6-millimeter keys should cover all the hex nut sizes used on your bike. A 1.5-millimeter key is required for micro adjustments on Shimano brakes.

Headset Wrench. One of the most common mountain bike problems is a loose headset. On most bikes, a single headset wrench is all that's needed to tighten the headset's locknut.

Cotterless Crank Bolt Wrench. Any alloy crank requires a tool to tighten the bolt that holds the crank to the spindle. Crank arms will loosen over a period of time and need to be checked regularly.

Third-Hand Tool. This gadget holds the brake pads against the rims so you can properly adjust your brakes. There's no universal third-hand tool, so you must find one that works properly with the type of cantilever brakes you have.

Cable Cutters. A good thing to have for replacing brake and derailleur cables and cable housing. Note: only a special Shimano cutter will cut index-shifting cable housing properly.

Spoke Wrench. These are used to tighten or loosen spokes in order to true a wheel. You have to make sure you get the particular wrench that fits the nipple size of the spokes on your wheels.

ADDITIONAL NEEDS

Chain Cleaner. Several companies (Vetta, Allsop, Park) make units that clean and/or clean and oil a chain in one simple operation. Try to clean and lube your chain at least once a week.

Toothbrush. When you replace your old toothbrush with a new one, keep the old one and put it in your bike repair kit. A toothbrush is invaluable for cleaning dirt and mud off those particularly hard-to-reach places.

Lubricant. Everyone has their favorite. Tri-Flow has been the standard for some time. Whatever the brand, synthetic lubricants with Teflon keep moving parts functioning properly and, unlike pure oils, are not prone to collecting dirt.

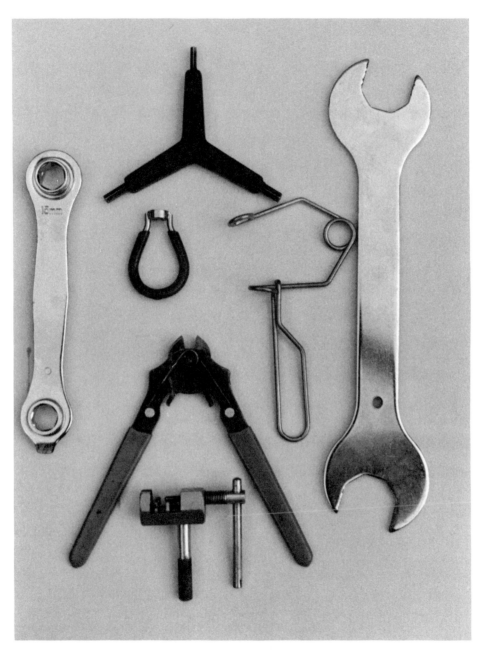

A basic home tool kit (clockwise from bottom): chain tool nestled between grips of cable cutters; cotterless crank bolt wrench; Allen key star tool; headset wrench. Inside: spoke wrench (left), third-hand tool (right).

Index Shifting

Cable tension is the key to accurate click shifting. Sometimes things go wrong—for example, when you shift from the second to the third cog but the chain shifts to the fourth cog. This indicates that cable tension has to be decreased.

The opposite is true if you find the shifts are not moving far enough. This is a common problem with new bikes, as shifter cables often stretch significantly when the bike is first used.

To fix an undershift problem, turn the small knob on the rear derailleur (located at the junction of the derailleur cable and the derailleur) or the knob on the right (rear) shifter counterclockwise to increase cable tension. To decrease tension, turn the knob(s) clockwise.

After any adjustment, take a test ride and be prepared to readjust if shifts made during the ride indicate that more or less tension is required.

Note, too, that often what appear to be derailleur problems are nothing more than gummed-up tension wheels causing the chain to skip (the tension wheels are the small cogged wheels of the rear derailleur). With a toothbrush soaked in solvent (I use ski wax remover), scrub the tension wheels clean every so often to keep your shifting sharp.

Shifter tension increases when you turn the tension knob counterclockwise, and decreases when you turn it clockwise.

On the trail, unwind the knob shown here to increase brake tension.

Brakes

On the trail, brakes can be tightened by turning the adjustment knob located where the brake cable meets the brake lever. As you open up (unwind the knob), brake tension increases. This is fine for a temporary fix. Never unwind the knob more than 50 percent of the total distance it can travel.

The best brake adjustment is done with the aid of a third-hand tool or a friend holding the brake pads against the rim. Begin by adjusting the brakes from the straddle cable clamp (the clamp that joins the straddle cable between the brakes with the main brake cable). Loosen the bolt and move the clamp up the main brake cable. Tighten the bolt and after loosening the third-hand tool or hand grip, try the brakes out. Make sure the brake tension knob is wound back down flush with the brake housing before making an adjustment.

Now if the straddle cable clamp adjustment doesn't do the job, the cable on the left brake arm (the fixed one, not the quick-release one) can be tightened by simply loosening the nut and pulling the cable down.

Generally a combination of these two adjustments will make your brakes tighter. If you ride a lot and do more than your share of descending, the brakes will have to be adjusted about once a month.

Often during adjustment or because of a heavy dose of downhill riding, the brake pads will slip off kilter. They can be adjusted by using a wrench, in conjunction with an Allen key, to loosen the brake pad arm assembly. Using a third-hand tool or a friend's helpful grip, clamp the brake shut and loosen the brake pad arm assembly. Then move the pads in or out, up or down.

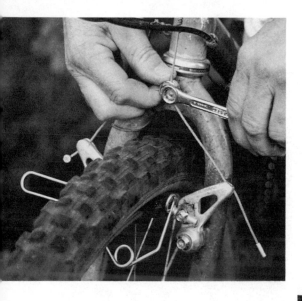

Brakes

With the help of a third-hand tool, adjust the straddle cable clamp.

You should also adjust brake cable tension at the brake arm.

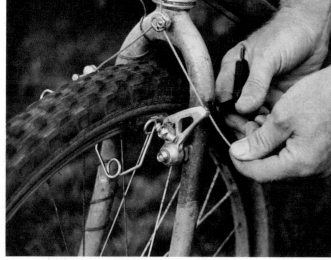

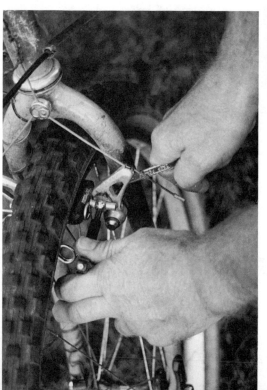

With a wrench and an Allen key, you can adjust the brake pads up or down, in or out.

Truing Wheels

If you ride off-road, the chances of your wheels staying true—without any wobbles—are slim. Bouncing along back roads and down rocky trails, the spokes work their way loose, and as their tension decreases, the wheel rim gets lopsided and the wheel wobbles.

Commercial bike shops use a truing stand as a guide to gauge the wheel's trueness. You can accomplish this at home by using your brake pads as the guides to detect where the wobbles are.

Standing, look down over the handlebars at the front brake's pads. Lift the front wheel up off the ground and spin it. As the wheel spins, squeeze the brake levers to bring the pads close to, but not in contact with, the rims. As an out-of-true portion of the wheel rim comes along, it will touch the pads. On the subsequent revolution, brake the wheel immediately after the rim hits the pads.

Having found an untrue section, tighten the spokes on the opposite side or loosen the spokes on the same side as the wobble. (It is better to tighten spokes when possible.)

Tightening is done with a spoke wrench (remember to get the right one for the nipple size of your spokes), turning the nipple clockwise. Start with a half turn, then continue to spin the wheel and check your progress until the wheel runs true.

Looking down from just behind the saddle, repeat the process to true the rear wheel.

When tightening spokes while truing a wheel, always start with a half turn clockwise.

Headset

Perhaps the most common problem with mountain bikes is a loose headset. Considering the combination of forces applied to the headset on a ride—rider weight on the handlebars, wheel banging over rough terrain—no wonder headsets work loose.

To remedy a loose headset, use your headset tool to loosen the locknut (it may already be loose), and then tighten the adjustable headset cone until you feel it making contact with the bearings. Then retighten the locknut.

After tightening, make the following tests to see if you've done the job correctly:

1. Apply the front brakes and jerk the handlebars back and forth to see if there's any looseness.

2. Next, let the wheel flop to the right or left. If it flops over easily, the headset is adjusted properly. If, however, the wheel doesn't flop at all or moves just a few inches, then the headset is too tight and the adjustable headset cone has to be loosened.

There are times when a loose headset becomes a chronic problem. If that occurs, try one of the following tricks:

1. Add a washer below the locknut.

2. Loosen the locknut, slide it up the stem, add some Loctite (blue) thread adhesive, and then bring the nut back down and tighten it. The Loctite should keep the nut from loosening.

To tighten a loose headset, use a wrench and turn it clockwise.

Another problem occurs when a reflector bracket is removed. This creates a gap that has to be filled with a spacer, or you'll have a loose headset problem.

Cranks

Periodically take a 5-millimeter Allen wrench and tighten the bolts that hold the chainrings together. After that, tighten the crank bolts with a thin-walled 14- or 15-millimeter socket wrench or specific crank arm tool.

Use a wrench to tighten a crank bolt (right), and an Allen key star tool to tighten the chainring bolts (below). As always, turn the tool clockwise.

Periodically check and tighten the handlebar clamp bolt.

A MINOR MAINTENANCE CHECKLIST

Perform the following on a regular basis to avoid troubles in the backcountry.

1. Make sure the bolt at the top of the stem and the one at its junction with the handlebars are tight.

2. Make sure the quick-releases on both wheels are on securely yet can be opened with pressure from the palm of the hand.

3. Make sure your seatpost quick-release is secure and that the bolts holding the saddle to the post are tight.

4. Make sure your toe clips are on snugly.

5. Make sure your pedals are tightly connected to the crank arm.

6. Make sure the bolts that hold the water bottle cages on are tight.

7. Make sure your pump works and that the spare tube you're carrying is in good shape. Packed tightly in an underseat pack, the tube's valve can puncture the main body of the tube.

ON THE ROAD

Prepare for any road trip by packing a few basic tools, all of which will fit into an under-the-saddle pack: Allen wrench set (4, 5, 6 millimeters), chain tool, spare links of chain, tube patch kit, spare tube, lubricant, tire levers/Quick-Stik, crank bolt wrench, combination flathead screwdriver and 10-millimeter wrench tool, hex set. Also take along a shop rag and a basic first-aid kit.

These tools should cover almost every emergency, from a flat tire to a broken chain.

Tools for the road (clockwise from top): lubricant, spare tube, crank bolt wrench, Allen key set, Quick Stik, hex set. Inside (clockwise from top): patch kit, chain tool, and combi flathead/10mm wrench tool.

Fixing a Flat

When it comes to troubles on the trail, flat tires are the number one problem. Here's the best procedure for fixing a flat:

1. Remove half of the tire bead with either two tire levers or a Quick-Stik tool.

2. Pull the old tube out.

3. Rub your hand around the inside of the tire to check for gravel or the end of a nail or staple sticking through.

4. Inflate your spare tube slightly (so it doesn't flop around) and insert it into the tire.

5. Put the tire bead back on the rim.

6. Inflate the tire partially; then spin the wheel slowly, checking to make sure the tire is properly seated.

7. Inflate the tire, and go on your way (or repair the tube first and put it in your pack before heading off again).

Fixing a Flat Tire

To fix a flat, start by prying
the bead off one side of the
tire (A, B), and remove the
tube.

A

B

Next, check to see if
whatever caused the flat is
visibly poking through the
tube or tire (C).

C

Inflate the spare slightly and insert it into the tire (D).

D

Then, refit the bead inside the rim (E).

E

Finally, inflate the spare to the desired pressure (F).

F

To understand your bike's workings to the utmost, set up a home shop and get into preventive maintenance.

Other Repair Problems

The next most common backcountry problem is a loose headset, which should be checked before you start your ride.

After a loose headset, there are brakes that can loosen during the ride. They can be quickly tightened by the procedure mentioned earlier.

Chains dry particularly easily in hot dusty weather or after a couple of stream crossings. When your chain starts to make a grating, rubbing noise, it's dry and is telling you it needs lubrication.

Other typical problems include the dreaded chain break. This is mountain biking's most overblown on-trail malfunction. In ten years of riding, I've experienced only two chain breaks.

When one occurs, use the chain tool to remove the faulty link (screw the chain tool arm through to push the pin holding the faulty link partially out). Then put the two chain ends back together (reversing the removal procedure). Some riders carry a section of chain in their repair kit and add as many links as needed to keep the chain at its proper length.

Without opening a Pandora's box of other possible trail repairs, I'll leave you with this piece of hard-earned, albeit hackneyed, wisdom: Truly expect the unexpected, and let necessity be the mother of your trailside repair inventiveness.

BOOKS

For those who wish to explore the depths of bicycle repair in general, I recommend Tom Cuthbertson's *Anybody's Bike Book* (Berkeley: Ten Speed Press, 1984). This is an easy read for nontechnical types and is mercifully free of the bike mechanics' mysticism that other manuals resort to.

For those who want to get right to the heart of mountain bike repairs, Dennis Coello's *Mountain Bike Repair Handbook* (New York: Lyons & Burford, 1990) is straightforward and easy to understand.

16

Trail Tips

The more you ride, the more you pick up ideas and tips on riding, what to take along, what to expect. Here are a few worth considering.

Workout Ratio. Most avid riders consider a 10-mile mountain bike ride the equivalent of a 25-mile road bike ride. That's not an absolute figure, but it illustrates the point that whenever you ride off-road, you work harder for each mile gained.

Beach Muscles. While I can't guarantee that you'll look like Arnold the Terminator after a year of active riding, it is a known fact that mountain bike riding is good upper body exercise. This is easy to understand when your arms are tired after a steep hill climb or a lift-and-lunge rocky descent. Then there are those lifts over fences, stream carries, and hoists of the bike on and off the car-top carrier.

Power Surges. A typical mountain bike ride is apt to consist of sudden explosive bursts of energy (an uphill climb, for example) followed by short rest periods. This is far different from road riding, where long intervals of steady cadence are followed by periods of short intensity.

Mountain biking's overall effect on the body is much like the effect a runner experiences in an interval workout: a combination of aerobic and anaerobic activity. This contrasts with road riding, where the cyclists gets more of an aerobic workout, similar to that of a distance runner.

Fluids for Function. There's no question that the most important item to carry along on any ride is water. Water is the mountain biker's power source.

239

Is mountain biking a great aerobic workout? You bet it is.

Add one of the many energy replacement compounds (Body Fuel, Exceed) to that water, and you'll find that it gives you a decided lift during a long tour or race. The energy replacement compounds help replace muscle sugars (glycogen) lost during exercise and keep you from "bonking" (running out of energy). A drink of water containing 2 percent simple sugar is equally effective and is used by many top athletes instead of the replacement compounds.

Fat Tire Food. Every rider has his or her favorite trail food. Since the creation of athletic energy bars (PowerBar, Fin-Halsa), you can get all the oomph you need in one small package. Three of either bar will keep a growing boy, hungry man, ravenous woman, full of energy on any half-day tour.

Quarter Pack. Somewhere in your repair kit, fanny pack, bike jersey, keep a quarter so you can telephone for help if something goes wrong (and if you can get to a phone).

Tour Checklist. Here's what you need for a fat-tire tour:

sleeping pad	eating utensils
sleeping bag	insect repellant
tent	sunscreen
change of clothes	water purification filter
change of shoes	Swiss Army knife
swim suit	first-aid kit
toiletry articles	
rain suit	*Optional:*
light sweater	cook stove
head lamp	cook pot set
repair kit	portable radio/tape player
spare tire	with earphones
spare spokes	books
map	light down jacket
snack food	baseball cap
three square meals	

Surprisingly, one athletic energy bar will power you along for miles and hours.

Message Service. When you leave home for any extended tour (three hours to multi-day), make sure you tell someone where you're going and when you you plan to be back. Having done this, the chances of your being found, if you get lost or hurt, are dramatically increased.

Glossary

A

Angling. Leaning the bike to one side or the other, with the front wheel steering straight ahead, in order to round a corner or dodge obstacles.

ATB. Acronym for All Terrain Bicycle. Some hoped ATB would become the generic term for the mountain bike—like the French VTT (*vélo de tout terrain*)—but it never took hold.

B

Bars. The short form of "handlebars"—nothing to do with saloons.

Bead. The portion of the tire that fits inside the wheel's rim. There are steel- and Kevlar-beaded tires; this refers to the reinforcing material used in the tire's bead.

Bonk. As in "on the bonk," or "he bonked": a term used to describe the dopey, punch-drunk feeling a cyclist gets when his energy resources run out during a ride.

Bottom bracket. The round tubing piece at the junction of the seat tube, down tube, and rear chainstays; it houses the axle and bearings. The height of the bottom bracket gives an idea of how much clearance the bike has; for example, an 11½-inch bottom bracket offers minimal clearance over logs and rocks, whereas a 13-inch bottom bracket offers a great deal of clearance. However, the higher the bottom bracket, the tippier and harder to handle the bike is apt to be.

Brake pads. The rubber-compound pads that press against the wheel's rim when the brakes are applied.

Braze-ons. Welded-on screw mounts that hold racks or water bottle cages.

243

Bunny hop. A maneuver in which the rider gets both wheels up off the ground with a short quick lift on the handlebars and pedals. Good for hopping over small obstacles at speed.

C

Cantilever brakes. The most popular type of mountain bike brakes, consisting of two independent brake arms linked by separate brake cables to a main brake cable.

Cantilever frame. A design popular on many balloon tire bikes of the 1940s and '50s, with an arcing top tube (or tubes in many cases) and an arcing down tube.

Chainrings. The three rings attached to the crank arm. The front derailleur moves the chain from one ring to another as you shift gears.

Chainstays. The two tubes that extend directly back from the bottom bracket and join, at the rear dropouts, with the seatstays.

Chain suck. This is what happens when, as the rider shifts onto the inner chainring, the chain goes slack for a moment and flies up and wedges between the inner chainring and the chainstay. Forward progress stops and brute force is required to extract the chain.

Clipless pedal systems. "Clipless" refers to the fact that no toe clips are required to keep the bike shoe securely on the pedal. With a clipless system, a special cleat attached to the shoe's sole mates with a specially designed receptacle pedal for a snug fit. Similar to a ski binding, it is released by a twist of the foot.

Cog. Any one of the multi-tooth gears that make up the freewheel.

Components. The parts of the bike (handlebars, gears, pedals, etc.)—essentially everything but the frame.

Crank arms. The bike's drive system, fitted with pedals at their ends and with chainrings on the right arm. Often referred to simply as cranks.

D

Death grip. When a rider grips the handlebars so tightly that his hands go numb, he is said to have a death—or better, scared to death—grip.

Derailleur. The mechanism that "derails" the chain and moves it to a new position. The front derailleur moves the chain over the chainrings; the rear derailleur moves the chain up and down the freewheel.

Down tube. The tube that angles down from the head tube to the bottom bracket.

Dropouts. The fork dropouts are the U-shaped ends of the fork, into which the axle of the wheel hub is inserted and clamped tight. The rear dropout is welded to the chainstay and seatstay.

Drum brake. Shaped like a drum, this brake encloses a wheel's hub. Brake shoes press against the inside of the drum to stop the bike. Drum brakes were popular in the early days of mountain biking, when riders converted old balloon tire bikes for off-road riding.

E

Eyelets. Brazed-on tabs with screw holes, installed on the forks and dropouts so that rear rack or fender struts can be attached to the bike frame.

F

Face plant. Any fall that results in a meeting of the face with the ground. Not a happy occasion and one to be avoided.

Forks. The tuning-fork-shaped front assembly that holds the front wheel.

Freewheel. The combination of cogs attached to the rear hub, generally denoted by the high/low gear ratio; for example, 12-26 for a cluster with a 26-tooth lowest gear ring and a 12-tooth highest gear ring. The gears in between 12 and 26 might be 14-, 16-, 18-, 20-, and 23-tooth for smooth shifting transitions.

G

Gear cluster. Same as "freewheel": a complete set of individual gear cogs put together to form 6- or 7-speed rear gearing.

Getting air. Flying through the air with both wheels well off the ground. A conscious pursuit of advanced riders.

Getting light. Essentially means staying loose in the saddle, ready for obstacles and changes in terrain, and when they occur being able to lightly pass through or over them.

Gnarly. The favored catchall adjective to describe any nasty descent, rough riding situation, tough ride, obnoxious person, intimidating terrain.

Granny gear. Either an ultra-small front chainring or large rear freewheel cogs, allowing the rider to make steep ascents.

H

Headset. This connects the front fork to the frame and allows the front wheel to steer.

Getting air.

Head tube. The short tube into which the front forks are inserted; it is attached to the down tube and top tube.

Hub. The center of each wheel, to which the spokes are attached. An axle runs through the hub to attach the wheel assembly to the frame.

K

Klunker, Klunking. In mountain biking's early days, any old bike that had been fixed up for off-road riding was called a klunker. Klunking was the nickname given to riding off-road.

L

Lift-and-lunge. The technique of lifting vigorously on the handlebars to pull the front wheel up to clear an obstacle, then lunging the body forward to drive the bike, and subsequently the rear wheel, over the obstacle.

P

Pannier. Literally, a saddlebag; used to describe the bags that attach to a rear or front rack, used for bike touring.

Picking a line. Looking over the terrain (most commonly a downhill) to select a route that allows the safest, fastest passage.

Pinch. Most flats in mountain bike tires are caused by pinches. A pinch occurs when a blow (hitting a rock, hole, curb) causes the tire to compress enough to pinch the tube between the rim and the tire. Pinches typically appear as two holes together, called a "snake bite."

Pounce. The position that has proven effective in ascending difficult terrain: a low forward lean with the rear slightly out of the saddle.

Q

Quick-release. A clamp device to hold a wheel hub or seatpost. It can be opened with a flick of the wrist to remove a wheel or, in the case of the seatpost, to raise, lower, or remove the post.

R

Racing bike. Generally, ultra-light, specially designed mountain bikes with steeper frame angles and state-of-the-art componentry. Racing bikes are built to go fast in the capable hands of expert riders.

Rake. The angle of the front fork—how far it is off the vertical. In conjunction with the head tube angle, fork rake helps determine how fast the bike steers and how stable it is overall.

Rear drop. A technique used to minimize rear wheel sideslip on descents. As the rider starts down a steep descent, he drops his rear off the back of the saddle. This lowers his center of gravity, weights the rear wheel, and keeps the rear wheel from wandering or lifting off the ground.

Riding the pegs. A term borrowed from motorcyclists and used to describe the out-of-the-saddle riding position in which the rider's weight rests mostly on his legs, with the pedals level, at the 3 and 9 o'clock positions.

Road bike. The common term for a traditional bike used for road riding and long-distance touring; also known as the 10-speed bike.

S

Saddle. The part of the bike you sit on.

Seatpost. The post that holds the bike seat; the other end meets the top tube and seat tube.

Seatstay. The two structural frame members that extend from the seat tube and join with the chainstays to form the bike's rear triangle.

Seat tube. The tube that extends directly up from the bottom bracket and houses the seatpost.

Shifter. The mechanism that allows you to shift both front and rear derailleurs. In the early days of mountain biking, it was up to the rider to push or pull the lever to get the gear he wanted, using "friction" shifters. Later "click" shifting came into being; it allows rider to click to the desired gear and the shift occurs almost automatically.

Until very recently, shifters had a single shifter lever and were mounted on top of the handlebars. Recently "push-push" shifters have been introduced. Located under the handlebars, they click from gear to gear, but instead of having to pull back on the shifter arm for some shifts, all shifts are done by forward pushes on one of the two shifter arms (one is for gearing up, one for gearing down).

Shifter cable. The cable that connects the shifter lever to its respective derailleur.

Slicks. Bald knobless tires used for on-road touring and slickrock riding.

Spin. To pedal at high revolutions in a low gear. This technique keeps the rider's legs limber and can help avoid the knee problems associated with pushing high gears.

Spindle. The axle that connects the crank arms.

Spinout. What happens when you apply power to your pedals only to have the rear wheel spin around without gripping the ground. Also can mean losing momentum when the bike slides out of control, as in "I spun out on that tight corner."

Stem. The L-shaped piece that extends straight up out of the headset and then juts forward, where it holds the handlebars. Stems come in different lengths and angles to help riders achieve the proper riding posture.

T

Technical section. A section of trail that requires bike-handling skills.

Top tube. The tube you straddle when you mount a bike; the one that forms the top of the bike's main triangle.

Touring bike. Generally, a road bike with a more conservative geometry and longer wheel base, designed to carry panniers and to be used for extended tours. Also can refer to a mountain bike set up with racks and slick tires for on-road touring.

Trials. (1) A competition in which riders ride an obstacle course that requires deft maneuvers and control at slow speeds; results are calculated on a combination of time and penalty points given for "dabs" (foot touching the ground for help). In most competitions, special small-frame, small-wheel, single-brake trials bikes are used. (2) Term used to describe a section of a ride that demands careful bike handling: "After the creek crossing, there was this nasty trials section."

True. You true a wheel when you adjust its spokes to eliminate the wobbles that occur naturally with use and as the spokes loosen.

Tuck. The aerodynamic body position used to maintain downhill speed: arms extremely bent, forehead almost touching the handlebars, body leaning far forward.

V

Valve stem. The piece through which a bike's inner tube is inflated. There are Schrader (car-type) and Presta (European-type) stems.

W

Walkover. The escape move used when the bike pitches the rider up over the

Popping a wheelie.